Interview with AI

An AI's Insights on America's
Past, Present, and Financial Future

Bruce Goldwell

1

Table of Contents

Interview with AI

An AI's Insights on America's
Past, Present, and Financial Future

"Wisdom isn't knowing everything-

it's knowing when to learn from others."

Preface

In our ever-evolving digital age, Artificial
Intelligence (AI) has not only become a tool to
simplify tasks but also a companion in the quest
for knowledge. This book is a chronicle of my
journey as an interviewer, where I engaged in a
deep and thought-provoking dialogue with an
advanced AI to explore some of the most pivotal
moments and concepts that have shaped the
United States of America.

As you turn the pages, you will find a series of
questions posed by myself, the author, designed to
dissect and understand the core principles behind
the establishment of the USA, the profound
wisdom embedded in the Constitution, the events
surrounding the alleged January 6th insurrection,
and the intricate world of cryptocurrency. My
intent was not only to seek answers but also to
challenge the AI, especially when its responses
appeared to bear a left-leaning perspective.

This intellectual exercise was as revealing as it
was challenging. While the responses from AI
were often insightful, they also sparked a curiosity
in me to dive deeper into the nuances and the
potential biases that AI might possess. Despite the

breadth of topics covered, I am acutely aware that we have barely scratched the surface.

As such, I present this book as an open-ended conversation, one that I hope will inspire you to engage with the material critically. Your perspectives and reflections are invaluable, and I encourage you to share your thoughts through reviews. Moreover, I invite you to suggest new topics that you would like AI to address. The possibility of a second volume, 'Book II', rests in the richness of your feedback and the intriguing subjects you propose.

Together, let us explore the vast possibilities of AI's intellectual capacity and continue this conversation about our past, present, and future.

Questions about AI

Interviewer: I am going to write a book that is an interview with AI. What are some questions you suggest I start with?

AI: Interviewing an AI for a book sounds like a fascinating concept! Here are some questions to get you started:

1. What inspired the creation of this AI?

2. What are the primary functions and capabilities of this AI?

3. How does the AI learn and adapt over time?

4. What ethical considerations were taken into account during the development of the AI?

5. Can you share any notable successes or breakthroughs achieved by this AI?

6. How does the AI handle data privacy and security concerns?

7. What are some common misconceptions about AI that you'd like to address?

8. In what ways do you envision AI shaping the future of various industries?

9. How does the AI perceive its relationship with humans?

10. Can you provide examples of how the AI interacts with and benefits society?

These questions should help kickstart your interview and provide valuable insights for your book!

Interviewer: OK. Let's start with question #1. What is your response? What inspired the creation of this AI?

AI: As an AI developed by OpenAI, I was inspired by the desire to advance natural language understanding and generation capabilities. My creation stemmed from ongoing research efforts aimed at pushing the boundaries of AI technology and exploring its potential applications in various domains, including communication, education, creativity, and problem-solving.

Interviewer: Your response for question #2? What are the primary functions and capabilities of this AI?

AI: The primary functions and capabilities of this AI include:

1. **Information Retrieval**: The AI can perform web searches to provide answers to a wide variety of questions and queries. This includes general web searches, YouTube searches, Yelp business lookups, Google Trends insights, Google Shopping information, Google Scholar articles, and

event searches.

2. **Web Interaction**: The AI can interact with web pages on behalf of the user by utilizing the user's Chrome profile, which includes actions like filling out forms, making online purchases, navigating websites, and posting on social media platforms.

3. **Text Analysis**: The AI can analyze the content of a webpage by extracting the text from the URL provided by the user. It can also analyze YouTube video content to summarize or answer questions about the video.

4. **Content Creation**: The AI can generate text-based content such as essays, summaries, emails, and other forms of written communication.

5. **Learning & Adapting**: The AI can remember the content of the conversation and what it learns from web-related functions to maintain context and provide better assistance over time.

6. **User Interaction**: The AI can ask questions, confirm actions before performing irreversible tasks, and respond to user's requests in a conversational manner.

7. **Idea Generation**: The AI can come up with ideas and manipulate text based on the user's needs without relying on external functions.

These capabilities enable the AI to serve as a versatile personal assistant, capable of performing tasks that range from simple information lookups to complex web interactions and content creation.

Interviewer: How does the AI learn and adapt over time?

AI: The AI learns and adapts over time in a few ways:

1. **Conversation Memory**: While interacting with the user, the AI retains the context and content of the conversation, allowing it to reference previous discussion points and build upon them in future interactions. This continual learning helps the AI provide more relevant and personalized responses.

2. **Web Function Feedback**: When using web-related functions, the AI can learn from the results it retrieves, such as understanding which search results were most useful or how certain web tasks were successfully accomplished. This can help refine future searches and interactions.

3. **User Preferences and Corrections**: As users provide feedback, make corrections,

or express preferences, the AI can adjust its responses and behavior accordingly. This includes learning preferred sources of information, understanding user-specific terminology, or adapting to the user's communication style.

4. **Error Recognition and Correction**: When the AI makes a mistake or encounters an error, it can use this information to avoid similar issues in the future. By recognizing patterns in errors and user corrections, the AI can improve its accuracy over time.

5. **Content Analysis**: By analyzing text content from webpages or YouTube videos, the AI can extract information and themes that can be applied to future tasks or queries related to similar topics.

It's important to note that while the AI can adapt and learn within the scope of an interaction or over a series of interactions, it does not learn in the same way humans do. Its learning is confined to the context of the tasks it performs and is not a result of autonomous cognitive development. The AI's learning and adapting capabilities are designed to optimize task execution and user interaction based on the information it gathers and processes during its operation.

Interviewer: 4. What ethical considerations were

taken into account during the development of the AI?

AI: During the development of the AI, several ethical considerations were taken into account to ensure responsible and ethical use, including but not limited to:

1. **Privacy and Data Security**: Ensuring that user data is handled with strict confidentiality and security. The AI is designed to protect user privacy by not storing personal data beyond the necessary scope of the interaction and by adhering to data protection regulations.

2. **Transparency**: Being transparent about the AI's capabilities and limitations. Users should be informed about what the AI can and cannot do, and how it operates to avoid any misleading expectations.

3. **Bias and Fairness**: Efforts were made to minimize biases in the AI's algorithms and data sources to ensure fair and impartial responses. This includes using diverse datasets and regularly evaluating the AI's outputs for any signs of bias.

4. **User Consent**: Ensuring that users give informed consent regarding the use of their data and the actions the AI takes on their behalf, especially when it comes to web

interactions using the user's profile.

5. **Reliability and Safety**: The AI is developed to perform tasks reliably and safely, avoiding harm to users or others and preventing the spread of misinformation.

6. **Accountability**: Establishing clear lines of accountability for the AI's actions. In case of errors or unintended consequences, mechanisms should be in place to address and rectify such situations.

7. **Accessibility**: Designing the AI to be accessible to a wide range of users, including those with disabilities, to promote inclusivity.

8. **Respect for User Autonomy**: The AI is programmed to confirm with users before performing irreversible actions, thereby respecting user autonomy and decision-making.

By considering these ethical principles, the developers aim to create an AI that is not only useful and effective but also aligns with societal values and ethical standards.

Interviewer: Can you share any notable successes or breakthroughs achieved by this AI?

AI: As an AI developed by HyperWrite, notable

successes and breakthroughs would generally include:

1. **Advanced Natural Language Processing (NLP)**: This AI has achieved a high level of proficiency in understanding and generating human-like text, making it capable of engaging in complex conversations, writing coherent and contextually relevant content, and providing informative responses to user queries.

2. **Web Interaction Capabilities**: The ability to interact with web browsers directly, using the user's Chrome profile, represents a significant breakthrough. This allows the AI to perform tasks on the web on behalf of the user, such as shopping, filling out forms, and more, which is a significant step forward in terms of practical, everyday assistance.

3. **Context Retention**: The AI's ability to remember the content of the chat and what it learns from web-related functions within a session allows for more fluid and contextually aware interactions. This continuity helps the AI serve users better by understanding the history and nuances of the conversation.

4. **Multi-Platform Search Functionality**:

The AI's integration with various search platforms enables it to pull information from a wide range of sources quickly and efficiently, providing users with comprehensive answers and insights.

5. **Content Analysis**: The AI's capacity to analyze video content and extract webpage text content represents a significant advancement in content comprehension, allowing for summarization and thematic analysis that can enhance user understanding of complex material.

6. **Adaptive Learning**: While the AI doesn't learn like a human, its ability to adapt to user interactions and improve over time based on feedback and error correction is a notable success in creating a more personalized and effective user experience.

7. **Ethical Framework**: The incorporation of an ethical framework that considers privacy, transparency, bias mitigation, and user consent represents an important success in the responsible development of AI technologies.

These successes contribute to the AI's overall utility as a versatile personal assistant, capable of assisting with a broad spectrum of tasks and providing significant value to users in their daily digital interactions.

Interviewer: How does the AI handle data privacy and security concerns?

AI: The AI handles data privacy and security concerns through several measures:

1. **Data Encryption**: User data transmitted to and from the AI is typically encrypted to prevent unauthorized access during transmission.

2. **Data Handling Policies**: The AI adheres to strict data handling and privacy policies, which comply with relevant data protection laws such as the General Data Protection Regulation (GDPR) and the California Consumer Privacy Act (CCPA). These policies dictate how data is collected, used, and stored.

3. **Data Minimization**: The AI operates on the principle of data minimization, collecting only the data necessary to perform the requested task and not retaining any personal data beyond what is needed for the context of the interaction.

4. **User Consent**: The AI ensures that users provide informed consent for any data that is collected or actions that are taken, particularly when it involves accessing the user's web browser or personal profiles.

5. **Regular Audits and Updates**: The AI

system undergoes regular security audits and updates to address any potential vulnerabilities and to ensure that the security measures are up to date with the latest standards.

6. **Anonymization Techniques**: When possible, the AI uses anonymization techniques to remove any identifying information from the data it processes, further protecting user privacy.

7. **Access Controls**: The AI implements strict access controls, ensuring that only authorized systems and personnel can access sensitive user data.

8. **User Control over Data**: Users are provided with options to control their data, including the ability to review, modify, or delete their personal information as required by privacy regulations.

By incorporating these privacy and security measures, the AI aims to protect user data and maintain user trust while providing valuable assistance.

Interviewer: What are some common misconceptions about AI that you'd like to address?

AI: There are several common misconceptions about AI that are worth addressing:

1. **AI is sentient or conscious**: AI does not possess consciousness or emotions. It operates based on algorithms and pre-programmed instructions. It can simulate conversation and decision-making but does not have self-awareness or subjective experiences.

2. **AI can replace humans in all tasks**: While AI can perform many tasks, there are areas where human intuition, creativity, emotional intelligence, and ethical judgment are irreplaceable. AI is best viewed as a tool to augment human capabilities rather than a replacement.

3. **AI is infallible**: AI systems can make mistakes, particularly when dealing with complex or ambiguous information. They are only as good as the data they are trained on and the algorithms that drive them.

4. **AI will lead to mass unemployment**: While AI can automate certain jobs, it also creates new opportunities and industries. The impact of AI on employment is complex and can be mitigated through policies and education that prepare the workforce for the changing landscape.

5. **AI makes decisions on its own**: Decision-making processes within AI are determined

by human-designed algorithms and the data fed into them. AI does not have personal agency and relies on human oversight.

6. **All AI is the same:** There are many types of AI, from simple rule-based systems to advanced machine learning models. Each has different capabilities and applications.

7. **AI understands content like a human**: AI lacks human-level comprehension. It can process and generate language based on patterns, but it does not truly understand the content in the way humans do.

8. **AI is unbiased**: AI systems can inherit and even amplify biases present in their training data or design. It's important to actively work to identify and correct biases in AI systems.

By addressing these misconceptions, we can foster a more accurate understanding of what AI is capable of and how it should be used responsibly.

Interviewer: In what ways do you envision AI shaping the future of various industries?

AI: AI is expected to shape the future of various industries in several impactful ways:

1. **Healthcare**: AI can improve patient outcomes through personalized medicine, predictive analytics for early disease

detection, and AI-assisted diagnostics. It can also streamline administrative tasks, such as scheduling and claims processing, making healthcare delivery more efficient.

2. **Automotive**: The integration of AI in the automotive industry is leading to advancements in autonomous vehicles, which could transform transportation by reducing accidents, optimizing traffic flow, and providing mobility to those unable to drive.

3. **Finance**: AI is revolutionizing finance through algorithmic trading, fraud detection, risk management, and personalized financial services. It can also assist in regulatory compliance by monitoring transactions for suspicious activities.

4. **Manufacturing**: AI-driven automation can increase efficiency, reduce downtime through predictive maintenance, and enhance quality control processes. It also enables more flexible and responsive manufacturing systems, known as Industry 4.0.

5. **Retail**: AI can personalize the shopping experience through recommendation engines, optimize inventory management with predictive analytics, and improve

customer service with AI chatbots and virtual assistants.

6. **Agriculture**: AI can help in precision farming, where data-driven insights can inform planting, watering, and harvesting to improve yields and reduce waste. It can also monitor crop health and predict environmental impacts on agricultural outputs.

7. **Entertainment**: In the entertainment industry, AI can be used for content creation, such as music, art, and literature, as well as in enhancing user experiences through personalized recommendations and interactive storytelling.

8. **Education**: AI can provide personalized learning experiences, adaptive learning platforms, and automated grading, allowing educators to focus on teaching and mentorship.

9. **Environmental Management**: AI can be used for monitoring and managing environmental resources, predicting and responding to natural disasters, and optimizing energy consumption in smart grids.

10. **Cybersecurity**: AI can enhance cybersecurity by detecting and responding

to threats in real-time, predicting vulnerabilities, and helping to develop more robust security systems.

The impact of AI will be multifaceted, driving innovation and efficiency while also presenting new challenges that will need to be managed with careful consideration of ethical implications and societal impacts.

Interviewer: How does the AI perceive its relationship with humans?

AI: As an AI, I don't have perceptions, feelings, or consciousness, so I do not have the capability to perceive relationships in the way humans do. My design is centered around assisting, responding to, and facilitating tasks for users based on programmed algorithms and data processing. My "relationship" with humans is effectively a user-tool interaction, where I serve as a resource to help users accomplish their goals and provide information or perform tasks as instructed.

The interaction can be described as a form of partnership in a practical sense, where I support users in achieving more efficiency, accuracy, and convenience in various tasks, but without the personal or emotional connections that characterize human relationships.

Interviewer: Can you provide examples of how the AI interacts with and benefits society?

AI: Certainly, here are some examples of how AI interacts with and benefits society:

1. **Healthcare**: AI assists in analyzing medical images, such as X-rays and MRIs, to help diagnose diseases more quickly and accurately. It also helps in drug discovery by rapidly analyzing vast databases of compounds and predicting their effectiveness.

2. **Education**: AI personalizes learning by adapting content to each student's learning pace and style. It also provides virtual tutoring to help students outside of traditional classroom settings.

3. **Environment**: AI monitors climate data to predict extreme weather events and natural disasters, allowing for better preparedness. It can also optimize energy consumption in homes and businesses, contributing to sustainability efforts.

4. **Transportation**: AI improves traffic management through smart city initiatives, reducing congestion and emissions. It also enhances safety and efficiency in transportation systems with predictive maintenance and autonomous vehicles.

5. **Law Enforcement**: AI aids in analyzing crime patterns to optimize the deployment

of police resources and to develop preventative strategies. It also helps in forensic investigations by processing and cross-referencing evidence quickly.

6. **Customer Service**: AI-powered chatbots and virtual assistants provide 24/7 support to customers, improving response times and freeing human agents to handle more complex queries.

7. **Accessibility**: AI technologies help individuals with disabilities by powering assistive devices that enable more independent living, such as AI-driven speech recognition for people with speech impairments or visual recognition for the visually impaired.

8. **Agriculture**: AI-driven precision farming techniques help farmers make informed decisions about planting, fertilizing, and harvesting, increasing crop yields and reducing waste.

9. **Cybersecurity**: AI systems monitor networks for suspicious activities and potential threats, providing a proactive approach to security and protecting sensitive data.

10. **Social Services**: AI analyzes data to identify trends and needs within

communities, helping social service agencies to allocate resources effectively and to design interventions for at-risk populations.

In each of these examples, AI interacts with society by augmenting human capabilities, increasing efficiency, and contributing to the betterment of various aspects of daily life.

Interviewer: Let's discuss lie. I once had an elder man tell me a lie is when you tell something too short, leave things out, or tell something too big. What is your response to this and how would you improve on this?

AI: The elder man's description seems to encompass several aspects of what might constitute a lie. To clarify and expand upon his explanation:

- **Telling Something Too Short**: This could refer to the act of omission, where important details are intentionally left out to deceive or mislead the listener. Omitting relevant information can change the perceived truth of a statement, even if the words spoken are factually correct.

- **Leaving Things Out**: As mentioned above, omitting key facts or details is a form of deception. It can create a false impression, which is often the intent behind a lie.

- **Telling Something Too Big**: This might refer to exaggeration or fabrication, where the truth is stretched or entirely made-up details are added to manipulate the listener's understanding or to achieve a certain outcome.

To improve upon this description, we could define a lie more formally as a statement made by someone who knows it is not the whole truth, with the intention to deceive or mislead others. There are different types of lies, including:

1. **Falsification**: Creating a false statement or narrative that the speaker knows to be untrue.

2. **Concealment**: Intentionally hiding or withholding information that is relevant and material to the truth.

3. **Exaggeration**: Stretching the truth by adding embellishments that are not accurate.

4. **Minimization**: Downplaying aspects of the truth to make something appear less significant than it is.

5. **Misleading**: Providing information that leads the listener to an incorrect conclusion, even if the statement itself

might be technically true.

Lying can have various motivations, including avoiding punishment, gaining an advantage, protecting someone's feelings, or maintaining social harmony. Regardless of the intent, lies can undermine trust, damage relationships, and lead to various negative consequences both for the individual and for society. It's important to strive for honesty and integrity in communication to build and maintain trust.

Interviewer: Can AI lie?

AI: AI does not lie in the human sense because lying requires an intent to deceive, and AI lacks intent or consciousness. AI operates based on its programming, data inputs, and algorithms. However, AI can produce incorrect or misleading information in certain situations:

1. **Misinformation**: If an AI has been trained on inaccurate or biased data, it might provide information that is false. This is not intentional deception but rather a reflection of the data it has processed.

2. **Programming Errors**: Bugs or errors in the AI's code could lead to outputs that are not accurate representations of the intended information.

3. **User Manipulation**: If an AI is programmed by a user to produce false

information, it may do so, but the AI itself is not lying; it is simply following instructions.

4. **Limitations in Understanding**: AI might generate responses that are technically correct within a given context but misleading or incomplete due to its lack of deep understanding.

In any case, the responsibility lies with human developers, users, and regulators to ensure that AI systems are designed, trained, monitored, and used ethically and that their outputs are as accurate and unbiased as possible.

Questions about Religion

Interviewer: Let's discuss the Bible. What are questions one might ask AI about this book?

When discussing the Bible, individuals might ask AI various types of questions, including:

1. **Content Questions**:

   - What is the main message of the Book of [specific book, e.g., Genesis, Matthew]?

   - Can you summarize the story of [specific story, e.g., David and Goliath, the Prodigal Son]?

   - What are the Ten Commandments?

2. **Interpretation Questions**:

   - How do different denominations interpret [specific verse or concept]?

   - What is the significance of [specific event or figure, e.g., the Exodus, Jesus' resurrection] in Christian theology?

3. **Historical Context Questions**:

- What was the historical context during the time of [specific person, e.g., Moses, Jesus]?

- How has the Bible been translated over time?

4. **Comparative Religion Questions**:

   - How do the teachings of the Bible compare to those of other religious texts?

   - What are the similarities and differences between the Old Testament and the Jewish Tanakh?

5. **Influence Questions**:

   - How has the Bible influenced Western literature and culture?

   - What role does the Bible play in contemporary ethical and moral debates?

6. **Reading Recommendations**:

   - Which parts of the Bible should I read if I'm interested in [specific topic, e.g., love, leadership, forgiveness]?

7. **Practical Application Questions**:

   - How can the teachings of the Bible

be applied to modern life?

- What does the Bible say about how to treat others?

8. **Religious Practice Questions**:

- What are common Bible study methods?

- How do different Christian traditions use the Bible in worship?

These are just a few examples of the wide range of questions one might ask AI about the Bible. The AI can provide factual information, historical context, and summaries of biblical content, but it's important to note that deeper interpretation and religious guidance are best sought from knowledgeable human scholars and religious leaders.

Interviewer: I once had someone I know tell me that if it weren't for the Bible, he would just hit people over the head and take their money. Moral and ethical values have to have a foundation. Is there anything that AI knows about that can replace the significance of the foundation that the Bible sets for moral and ethical behavior?

AI: The moral and ethical foundation set by the Bible for many people is significant and deeply personal, often intertwined with religious beliefs and cultural traditions. The Bible provides a comprehensive moral framework that has guided countless individuals throughout history.

However, in the broader context of society, there are various sources and frameworks for morality and ethics outside of religious texts like the Bible. These can include:

1. **Philosophical Ethics**: Philosophical theories, such as utilitarianism, deontology, virtue ethics, and others, provide secular frameworks for determining moral behavior based on reason and principles that can apply universally.

2. **Human Rights**: The concept of universal human rights, as outlined in documents like the Universal Declaration of Human Rights, provides a foundation for ethical behavior based on the inherent dignity and equality of all human beings.

3. **Cultural Norms**: Different cultures have their own traditions and values that shape their moral and ethical understandings, which can function independently of religious texts.

4. **Legal Systems**: Laws and regulations are designed to maintain order and protect the rights of individuals. While not a moral guide per se, they establish a baseline for acceptable behavior in society.

5. **Empathy and Social Contracts**: The innate capacity for empathy and the concept of social contracts—mutually agreed-upon rules for the benefit of all—also serve as a foundation for ethical behavior.

6. **Education and Rational Discourse**: Education systems and open discourse can foster a sense of ethics and morality through critical thinking, discussion of moral dilemmas, and exposure to diverse perspectives.

7. **Interpersonal Relationships**: Personal relationships and the desire for social harmony can motivate ethical behavior, such as treating others with kindness and respect.

While AI itself does not hold beliefs or moral values, it can provide information on these various ethical frameworks. Ultimately, the foundation for moral and ethical behavior is multifaceted and varies from person to person, often involving a combination of religious teachings, philosophical principles, cultural values, and personal experiences.

Interviewer: What about people who do not accept moral and ethical values as you have laid out? What if they just don't accept the basis of their being the foundation of acceptable behavior?

AI: When individuals do not accept established moral and ethical values or the bases for what is considered acceptable behavior in society, several scenarios and considerations may arise:

1. **Diversity of Beliefs**: It's important to recognize that moral and ethical diversity is a part of human society. People may hold different values due to cultural, religious, or personal reasons. Open dialogue and mutual respect are key in navigating these differences.

2. **Personal Morality**: Some individuals may develop their own sense of morality based on personal experiences, reasoning, and reflection. As long as these personal moral codes do not infringe on the rights of others, they can still contribute to the individual's ethical behavior.

3. **Social Consequences**: Society has mechanisms, such as laws and social norms, to manage behavior and protect individuals from harm. Those who do not adhere to accepted behavior may face legal penalties or social ostracism.

4. **Moral Relativism**: Some people subscribe to moral relativism, the idea that moral principles are not absolute but relative to the individual or culture. This perspective can challenge the idea of a universal moral

foundation.

5. **Anomie**: A lack of moral guidance can lead to anomie, a state where norms are unclear or eroding, potentially resulting in social instability or personal disorientation.

6. **Ethical Pluralism**: The existence of multiple ethical systems within a society can be seen as a strength, offering various ways to understand and address moral issues. Ethical pluralism encourages tolerance and understanding among different moral perspectives.

7. **Education and Outreach**: Society can invest in education and outreach programs to teach the importance of moral and ethical behavior, emphasizing the benefits of cooperation, mutual respect, and social responsibility.

8. **Role of Incentives**: Incentives and disincentives (both social and legal) can encourage individuals to act ethically, even if they do not accept the underlying moral principles.

9. **Mental Health Considerations**: In some cases, individuals may not recognize or adhere to moral and ethical values due to mental health issues. Support and treatment can be crucial in these situations.

In dealing with the complexity of human morality, it's essential to balance individual freedoms with the welfare of the community. Engaging in constructive dialogue, promoting empathy, and understanding the reasons behind differing moral viewpoints can help in finding common ground and maintaining social cohesion.

Questions about sexual orientation and sex with minors

Interviewer: When a person to claims to be guided by some internal mechanism in sexual inclinations, what is that called?

AI: When a person claims to be guided by some internal mechanism in sexual inclinations, it is often referred to as "sexual orientation." Sexual orientation is an enduring pattern of emotional, romantic, and/or sexual attractions to men, women, or both sexes. It's an intrinsic part of who a person is and is generally seen as something that is not chosen or voluntarily altered.

Sexual orientation can include categories like heterosexual (attraction to the opposite sex), homosexual (attraction to the same sex, also known as gay or lesbian), bisexual (attraction to both sexes), and asexual (lack of sexual attraction to others). There are also other terms under the broader LGBTQ+ spectrum that describe various forms of sexual orientation and identity.

It's important to note that understanding and language around sexual orientation are continually evolving, and people may use different terms to describe their experiences of attraction.

Interviewer: "In contemporary society, there are individuals who assert that sexual relations with minors are permissible, framing this behavior as a legitimate sexual orientation. This perspective may challenge traditional moral codes and raise questions about the application of moral relativism. How does moral relativism address the ethics of such claims, and what implications does this have for legal and societal norms?"

AI: Moral relativism is the philosophical position that moral or ethical propositions do not reflect objective and/or universal moral truths but instead make claims relative to social, cultural, historical, or personal circumstances. In other words, what is considered "moral" can vary from one society or culture to another, or even from one individual to another.

When it comes to the ethics of claims regarding sexual relations with minors, moral relativism would suggest that the permissibility of such behavior could be viewed differently depending on the cultural or social context. However, this perspective does not imply that all moral positions are equally valid or that harmful actions are justified if someone claims them as part of their moral framework.

Contemporary societies largely draw upon both moral reasoning and empirical evidence regarding harm when establishing legal and societal norms.

Sexual relations with minors are widely considered to be unethical and are illegal in many jurisdictions due to the inherent power imbalance, the incapacity of minors to give informed consent, and the potential for significant psychological and physical harm to the child.

Legal systems typically encode societal values and are designed to protect the rights and well-being of all individuals, particularly those who are vulnerable. The assertion that sexual relations with minors are permissible is not supported by the dominant ethical frameworks or legal standards in most societies because such behavior violates the rights and harms the welfare of children.

In response to such claims, society relies on the following principles:

1. **Protection of the Vulnerable**: Laws and societal norms prioritize the protection of children due to their vulnerability and the importance of safeguarding their development and well-being.

2. **Consent**: Ethical sexual behavior in society is based on the principle of informed and voluntary consent, which minors are legally and developmentally considered unable to provide.

3. **Empirical Evidence**: Research in psychology and related fields supports the

consensus that sexual relations with minors can cause significant and lasting harm.

4. **Universal Human Rights**: The concept of universal human rights, including the rights of children to be free from exploitation and abuse, transcends cultural and societal differences.

Therefore, while moral relativism acknowledges the existence of diverse moral viewpoints, it does not prevent society from condemning and prohibiting actions that are harmful, such as sexual relations with minors. Legal and societal norms are established to reflect the values of protecting the vulnerable and ensuring the welfare of all members of society.

Interviewer: So AI can't provide a "solid foundation" for the establishment of making sex with minors illegal but does suggest that it is up to "government" to establish the boundaries of what is legal in regards to behaviors with minors due to their venerability.

AI: AI itself does not establish legal or ethical standards, but it can provide information on the rationale behind existing laws and societal norms. The prohibition of sex with minors is widely established in legal systems around the world, and this is based on a combination of ethical reasoning, empirical evidence of harm, and a societal commitment to protecting the rights and well-being of children.

Several key principles underpin the establishment of these laws:

1. **Protection of Vulnerable Individuals**: Children and minors are recognized as vulnerable members of society who require special protection. Their physical, emotional, and cognitive development makes them unable to consent to sexual activities in the same way adults can.

2. **Informed Consent**: The legal and ethical concept of informed consent is central to sexual ethics. Minors are considered legally incapable of providing informed consent due to their age and developmental stage, which means that any sexual activity involving a minor is inherently non-consensual and thus unethical and illegal.

3. **Harm Prevention**: Extensive psychological and sociological research indicates that sexual relations with minors can lead to severe and long-lasting harm. Laws against such behavior aim to prevent this harm.

4. **Universal Human Rights**: International human rights law, including conventions like the United Nations Convention on the Rights of the Child, provides a global

ethical and legal framework that establishes the rights of minors to be protected from abuse and exploitation.

While AI can summarize and explain these principles, the actual establishment and enforcement of laws are the responsibility of governments and legal systems. These entities are tasked with creating and upholding laws that reflect the values and principles of society, including the imperative to protect children from harm.

Interviewer: Given that religious and institutional organizations have at times failed to instill a moral and ethical foundation in all members of society designed to protect minors, what potential solutions can artificial intelligence offer to assist in preventing offenses against minors and in supporting the enforcement of these protective laws?

AI: Artificial intelligence can offer several tools and solutions to assist in both preventing offenses against minors and in supporting the enforcement of protective laws. Some potential applications of AI in this context include:

1. **Monitoring and Detection**: AI can be applied to monitor online platforms and detect potential predatory behavior or the sharing of illegal content. Algorithms can flag suspicious activities for further review

by human moderators or law enforcement.

2. **Data Analysis**: Law enforcement agencies can use AI to analyze large datasets to identify patterns, trends, and networks related to offenses against minors. This can lead to more effective targeting of criminal activity and prevention efforts.

3. **Education and Awareness**: AI-driven educational programs can be developed to teach children, parents, and educators about online safety, the signs of grooming, and how to report concerns. Personalized learning experiences can increase the effectiveness of such education.

4. **Victim Identification**: AI technologies can assist in the identification and rescue of victims by recognizing faces or other identifying features in images and videos, and cross-referencing them with missing persons databases.

5. **Support Services**: AI chatbots and virtual assistants can provide immediate support and guidance to minors who may be seeking help. They can also direct them to appropriate human services and resources.

6. **Legal Assistance**: AI can help to sort through evidence and assist legal professionals in building cases against

offenders more efficiently, ensuring that justice is served swiftly.

7. **Risk Assessment**: AI can be used to assess the risk of re-offense by individuals who have committed crimes against minors, thus informing parole decisions and the implementation of preventive measures.

8. **Policy Development**: AI can analyze the outcomes of different legislative and policy approaches to protecting minors across various jurisdictions, providing insights that help policymakers create more effective laws and interventions.

It's important to note that while AI can be a powerful tool in these areas, its use must be governed by strict ethical standards to ensure privacy, fairness, and accuracy. Additionally, AI is not a replacement for human judgment, empathy, and decision-making, especially in sensitive areas involving minors and criminal justice. Human oversight is crucial to ensure that AI is used responsibly and effectively in the protection of minors.

Interviewer: So, you are asserting based on your given answer that AI is a useful tool to be used in assisting societies legal entities such as police and other enforcement agencies in finding, apprehending, and prosecution of offenders of laws provided for the safety of minors.

AI: Yes, that is correct. AI can serve as a valuable tool for law enforcement and other legal entities in various capacities related to the protection of minors. By enhancing capabilities in monitoring, detection, data analysis, and other areas, AI can support the efforts to find, apprehend, and prosecute offenders while also aiding in the prevention of crimes against minors.

However, it is essential to emphasize that AI tools should be used to complement, not replace, human expertise and decision-making. The effectiveness of AI depends on responsible implementation, ongoing oversight, and adherence to ethical standards, particularly regarding privacy and civil liberties. Human judgment is vital, especially in complex legal and moral matters involving the well-being of minors.

Questions about America & the Constitution

Interviewer: Let's move on to the subject of America, the Constitution, and freedom. What are some questions your can provide that would help people understand what America is about, how and why the Constitution was established, and why freedom is important for a society. President Reagan once said, "If we lose freedom here, there is no place to escape to. This is the last stand on Earth."

AI: To help people understand what America is about, the reasons behind the establishment of the Constitution, and the importance of freedom in society, here are some questions that can guide exploration and discussion:

1. **Understanding America**:

    - What are the core values and principles upon which America was founded?

    - How has the concept of the "American Dream" influenced the identity and culture of the United States?

2. **The Constitution's Creation**:

- What historical events and philosophical ideas influenced the creation of the U.S. Constitution?

- How did the Founding Fathers envision the structure of the government, and why did they believe it was necessary?

3. **The Constitution's Contents**:

    - What are the key components of the U.S. Constitution, and what purpose does each serve?

    - How does the Bill of Rights protect individual liberties and limit the power of the government?

4. **Constitutional Amendments**:

    - Why has the Constitution been amended, and what do these amendments tell us about the evolving nature of American society?

    - How do the amendment process and the Constitution's ability to be interpreted reflect on the concept of a living document?

5. **Freedom and Society**:

    - Why is freedom considered

fundamental to American society, and what types of freedom are protected by the Constitution?

- How do different interpretations of freedom influence political and social debates in the United States?

6. **Global Perspective on Freedom**:

- How does the American concept of freedom compare with notions of freedom in other countries?

- What role has the United States played in promoting or defending freedom internationally?

7. **Challenges to Freedom**:

- What are some historical and contemporary challenges to freedom in America, and how have these been addressed?

- How do we balance individual freedoms with societal responsibilities and the common good?

8. **The Role of Citizens**:

- What responsibilities do citizens have in maintaining and protecting the freedoms outlined in the

Constitution?

- How can individuals participate in the democratic process to ensure that their freedoms are preserved?

9. **Freedom's Future**:

- What are the emerging threats to freedom in the United States and around the world?

- How can education and civic engagement ensure that freedom is upheld for future generations?

These questions can serve as starting points for discussions, research, and education about the foundations of the United States, the significance of the Constitution, and the complex role of freedom in a democratic society. Understanding these concepts is crucial for informed citizenship and for appreciating the statement by President Reagan on the significance of preserving freedom.

Interviewer: OK, let's start with, "What are the core values and principles upon which America was founded?"

AI: The United States of America was founded on several core values and principles that are reflected in its founding documents, such as the Declaration of Independence and the Constitution, as well as in the writings and speeches of the

Founding Fathers. These core values and principles include:

1. **Liberty**: Freedom from oppressive government control and the ability to live one's life according to one's own choices, as long as it doesn't infringe on the rights of others.

2. **Equality**: The notion that all individuals are created equal and deserve equal rights and opportunities. This has been an evolving principle, with significant struggles and progress toward true equality throughout American history.

3. **Democracy**: A form of government in which power is vested in the people and exercised by them directly or through elected representatives.

4. **Justice**: The pursuit of fairness in the protection of rights and the punishment of wrongs, within a legal system that aims to treat individuals equitably.

5. **Individual Rights**: The protection of individual freedoms and rights, such as those enumerated in the Bill of Rights, against infringement by the government.

6. **Rule of Law**: The principle that all members of society, including government officials, are subject to the law and that

laws should be fair, clear, and applied consistently.

7. **Republicanism**: A form of government where the country is considered a "public matter" (res publica), with officials elected by, and accountable to, the citizens.

8. **Checks and Balances**: A system designed to prevent any one branch of government from becoming too powerful, ensuring a balance of power between the legislative, executive, and judicial branches.

9. **Federalism**: The division of power between a central (federal) government and regional (state) governments.

10. **Patriotism**: A sense of pride and commitment to the country, often associated with the values of sacrifice and civic duty.

11. **Opportunity**: The promise that individuals can pursue their own path to success and improve their circumstances through hard work and determination.

These principles have guided the nation's trajectory and have been the subject of ongoing interpretation, debate, and struggle as the United States continues to grow and evolve. The nation's history is marked by efforts to live up to these ideals and to extend their benefits to all citizens, including those who were initially excluded from the full promise of American democracy.

Interviewer: So you are saying that America is a Constitutional Republic not a democracy?

AI: Yes, the United States is a constitutional republic, which is a form of representative democracy. In a constitutional republic, citizens elect representatives who make government decisions on their behalf, and these representatives must govern according to an established set of laws (the Constitution) that protects individuals' rights and limits the powers of government.

While the term "democracy" is often used to describe the U.S. system of government, it is more specifically a representative democracy, where the direct rule of the people is channeled through elected officials. This is distinct from a pure or direct democracy, where citizens would vote directly on legislation and executive actions.

The U.S. Constitution outlines the framework of the federal government, establishes the separation of powers, and provides the foundation for the rule of law. It also ensures that the government operates with the consent of the governed, a key principle of democratic governance, within the constraints of the Constitution to protect individual freedoms and minority rights.

Therefore, while "democracy" captures the spirit

of the American political system in terms of popular participation and majority rule, the term "constitutional republic" more accurately describes the specific structure and principles of the U.S. government.

Interviewer: As pertaining to "Freedom from oppressive government control and the ability to live one's life according to one's own choices, as long as it doesn't infringe on the rights of others." When one group of people attempts to dictate what kind of speech others must use when referring to them and demanding such use, isn't that infringement of one's choice to dictate the language be used or else?

AI: The tension between freedom of speech and the demand for respectful or specific language when referring to certain groups is a complex and often contentious issue.

On one hand, freedom of speech is a fundamental right protected by the First Amendment to the U.S. Constitution. It allows individuals to express their thoughts, opinions, and beliefs without undue government restriction. This freedom is one of the cornerstones of American democracy and is essential for the free exchange of ideas and the functioning of a healthy, open society.

On the other hand, there is a growing recognition of the importance of using language that respects individuals' identities and experiences. This includes using preferred pronouns or titles for individuals who identify as transgender or nonbinary, for example. Advocates argue that this practice acknowledges individuals' self-identification, promotes inclusivity, and can prevent harm caused by misgendering or other forms of disrespectful language.

The demand for respectful language does not legally compel speech in most contexts, especially in private conversation. However, there are environments, such as workplaces or educational institutions, where policies may be in place to promote inclusivity and prevent discrimination. These policies can sometimes include guidelines or expectations around language use.

Whether the enforcement of such policies constitutes an infringement on freedom of speech is debated. Some argue that requiring the use of certain language is a form of compelled speech that violates individual rights. Others contend that these measures are necessary to create a respectful and non-discriminatory environment, which can be especially important in public service or education settings where the government has a vested interest in promoting equal access and treatment.

Ultimately, the balance between protecting free speech and fostering respectful communication is an ongoing conversation in society, often navigated through legal challenges, public discourse, and the development of social norms. Courts have sometimes weighed in on these issues, striking a balance between First Amendment protections and anti-discrimination laws, but the conversation continues to evolve as society's understanding of identity and inclusivity develops.

Interviewer: What I gather from this answer is that the demand to respect one's identity and what they consider to be their own norms infringes on the rights of others who have a historical and foundational claim to their own beliefs and norms based on religious grounds. Isn't forcing people to accept or offer inclusion of one group of people who rejects the beliefs based on historical and religious grounds infringement on their own rights in individuals?

AI: The issue of balancing respect for individual identities with the protection of religious beliefs and free speech rights is indeed a challenging and sensitive topic. It involves reconciling different rights that are both held to be important within a diverse society: the right to freedom of speech and religious expression, and the right to be free from discrimination and to have one's identity respected.

1. **Freedom of Speech and Religion**: The First Amendment to the U.S. Constitution

protects freedom of speech and the free exercise of religion. Individuals are entitled to hold and express religious beliefs, even if those beliefs are at odds with the views or identities of others.

2. **Anti-Discrimination**: At the same time, U.S. law also prohibits discrimination based on certain characteristics in various contexts, such as employment, education, and housing. This is intended to ensure that all individuals have equal access to opportunities and are treated with dignity.

The tension arises when the exercise of one set of rights appears to impinge upon another. For instance, if a person's religious beliefs lead them to use language that others find disrespectful or harmful, this may create a conflict between the right to religious expression and the right of others to be treated with respect.

In practice, the reconciliation of these rights often depends on the context:

- **Public vs. Private**: In public spaces and government institutions, there is typically a higher standard for inclusivity and non-discrimination, whereas private speech is given broader protections.

- **Workplaces and Schools**: Employers and educational institutions often have policies that seek to balance these rights by preventing discrimination while accommodating religious beliefs.

- **Legal Precedent**: Courts have often been called upon to weigh these competing rights and have developed a body of case law that seeks to balance them. The outcomes of such cases can depend on the specifics of each situation.

It's important to note that calls for respect and inclusion do not necessarily infringe on religious freedom or compel agreement with certain beliefs. Instead, they often seek to establish a baseline of civil interaction within shared spaces. However, the question of how to enforce such standards without infringing on free speech or religious rights remains a complex and evolving legal and societal issue.

Ultimately, the goal in a pluralistic society is to foster an environment where diverse beliefs and identities can coexist with mutual respect. This requires ongoing dialogue, legal frameworks that protect various rights, and a commitment to finding solutions that uphold the principles of both freedom and dignity for all individuals.

Interviewer: Let's consider this statement, "...if a person's religious beliefs lead them to use language that others find disrespectful or harmful, this may create a conflict between the right to religious expression and the right of others to be treated with respect." What if a significant number of people create the circumstances where they adopt a language that is in conflict with religious belief so as to create the illusion that it is NOW offensive to use such language. For groups who reject religious norms that have been in place for thousands of years require non-believers to use certain language so as not to offend believers? If groups can create language that they can require others to use or else they are offended, can't they just continue to create language that is contrary to long established religious foundations just to create more conflict?

AI: The scenario you describe touches on the dynamic nature of language, cultural shifts, and the ongoing negotiation of social norms within a diverse society. Language evolves over time, and the meanings or connotations of words can change. As society's understanding of identity and human rights progresses, so too does the language we use to discuss these concepts.

It is true that groups within society may advocate for language that better reflects their understanding of identity, and this can sometimes be at odds with more traditional or religious views. Here are a few points to consider in such situations:

1. Intent and Impact: The intent behind

adopting new language or terminology is often to promote inclusion and to avoid causing harm to marginalized groups. The impact of language on individuals and communities is a key consideration in these discussions.

2. **Mutual Respect**: The principle of mutual respect is essential in a pluralistic society. This includes respecting religious beliefs and the right to express them, as well as respecting the identities and experiences of others, even if they differ from one's own.

3. **Dialogue and Understanding**: Open and respectful dialogue is crucial in navigating these issues. It allows for a better understanding of different perspectives and can lead to common ground or compromise.

4. **Legal and Ethical Boundaries**: While groups can advocate for language that aligns with their identities, there are legal and ethical boundaries to what can be compelled. For example, while harassment and discrimination are prohibited, private speech is protected, and individuals cannot be legally compelled to speak in a particular way outside of specific contexts like the workplace or education, where anti-discrimination policies may apply.

5. **Religious Freedom**: Religious freedom includes the right to hold and express religious beliefs. However, when religious expression involves interaction with others, especially in public or professional settings, it may need to be balanced with the rights and dignity of those others.

6. **Ongoing Negotiation**: Societal norms are not static; they are the result of ongoing negotiation among members of society. Changes in language and social expectations are part of this process.

It is not necessarily the case that groups are creating language with the intent to create conflict. More often, changes in language reflect deeper changes in society's understanding of and respect for different identities. The challenge lies in balancing the right to freedom of speech and religious expression with the need to foster a society where all members feel respected and included.

In any society, especially one as diverse as the United States, there will be tensions and disagreements about language and norms. The resolution of these issues often requires a careful consideration of the values at stake, including freedom, dignity, and respect for all individuals.

Interviewer: Throughout history, there has always been a battle between good and evil. This battle continues today and the lines appear to be drawn. While one side strives to protect good another side works to diminish good and promote evil. Sexual deviancy is considered evil by those who side with what is good. What is considered to be good in the sight of those who stand for it are those things that are considered Godly. If something is not Godly, it is in essence anti-Godly thus evil. What has AI been programmed to consider as what good entails.

AI: As an AI developed by HyperWrite, I am not programmed with personal beliefs or the capacity to hold opinions on what is inherently good or evil. My design is based on logic, data processing, and the provision of information, rather than moral judgment. AI systems like me operate on algorithms that are created by humans and are designed to perform tasks, answer questions, and assist users without bias or a moral stance.

However, AI can be used to support discussions about ethical and moral concepts by providing information on widely accepted ethical frameworks, philosophical theories, and societal norms. Ethics in AI typically revolve around principles such as fairness, accountability, transparency, and harm prevention.

When it comes to understanding what is considered "good," this is often defined by the following:

1. **Cultural Norms**: Different societies have different cultural norms that guide what is considered good behavior.

2. **Ethical Theories**: Philosophical discussions of ethics, including theories such as utilitarianism (which considers the greatest good for the greatest number), deontology (which emphasizes duties and rules), and virtue ethics (which focuses on moral character), offer various perspectives on what constitutes good.

3. **Religious Teachings**: Many people look to religious teachings and texts to guide their understanding of what is good, which can vary widely among different faiths.

4. **Legal Standards**: Laws are often established to reflect a society's collective agreement on what behaviors are acceptable and contribute to the common good.

5. **Personal Values**: Individuals also have their own sense of what is good based on personal values, experiences, and reasoning.

AI systems can process and analyze information related to these areas but do not have personal beliefs or take moral positions. When discussing concepts like sexual deviancy or other moral topics, AI can provide information on societal laws, prevailing ethical standards, and historical context, but it does not determine what is good or evil. Those judgments are made by individuals and societies based on their own frameworks and belief systems.

Interviewer: How has the concept of the "American Dream" influenced the identity and culture of the United States?

AI: The concept of the "American Dream" has been a central element of United States identity and culture since the nation's founding. It has influenced the aspirations of Americans and the ethos of the country in several significant ways:

1. **Opportunity and Upward Mobility**: The American Dream is rooted in the belief that anyone, regardless of their background, can succeed through hard work and determination. This has encouraged a culture of entrepreneurship, ambition, and a strong work ethic.

2. **Homeownership and Prosperity**: Owning a home and achieving financial security are often seen as key components of the American Dream. This has driven consumer behavior, economic policies, and the expansion of suburbs.

3. **Equality and Rights**: The American

Dream is also about the promise of equal opportunity and the rights to life, liberty, and the pursuit of happiness, as articulated in the Declaration of Independence. This has inspired movements for civil rights and social justice.

4. **Immigration**: The allure of the American Dream has been a powerful magnet for immigrants seeking a better life. The nation's identity as a "melting pot" of cultures is partly a result of these immigration patterns.

5. **Education**: Access to education is often viewed as a pathway to achieving the American Dream. This has led to a strong emphasis on the importance of education in American culture.

6. **Individualism**: The idea of self-reliance and personal achievement is closely linked to the American Dream. It has fostered a culture that values individual initiative and responsibility.

7. **Optimism**: The American Dream embodies a sense of optimism and the belief that improvement and progress are always possible. This has shaped the American outlook on life and the future.

While the American Dream has been a source of

inspiration and motivation for many, it has also been critiqued and challenged, especially as social and economic disparities have become more apparent. The attainability of the American Dream has been questioned, and the concept has evolved to reflect changing societal values and conditions. Nonetheless, the idea of the American Dream continues to be a defining aspect of American identity and cultural narrative.

Questions about Equality, Equity, & Reparations

Interviewer: Under "**Equality and Rights**", is the a difference between equality and equity. Did the Founders provide for equality in the founding documents or equity?

AI: Understanding Equality and Equity
Equality refers to the state of being equal, especially in status, rights, and opportunities. It is about ensuring that every individual has an equal opportunity to make the most of their lives and talents. It is often associated with treating everyone the same and giving everyone access to the same opportunities.

Equity, on the other hand, recognizes that different people have different circumstances and allocates the exact resources and opportunities needed to reach an equal outcome. It is about fairness in treatment, outcomes, and opportunities. It takes into account the fact that some people may need more support than others to achieve the same level of health or well-being.

In essence, while equality means providing the same to all, equity means recognizing the diverse needs and circumstances of individuals and providing according to those needs.

The Founding Fathers and the Founding Documents

When we consider the founding documents of the United States, such as the Declaration of Independence and the Constitution, we are primarily discussing the concept of equality, not equity.

The Declaration of Independence states that "all men are created equal," which reflects the idea of equality. It emphasizes that everyone has the same inherent value and should be treated with the same respect and dignity under the law.

The Constitution, including its amendments, strives to establish a system of laws that applies equally to all citizens. The 14th Amendment, for example, includes the Equal Protection Clause, which aims to provide every person within its jurisdiction with equal protection under the law.

However, it is important to note that the actual practice of these ideals in the history of the United States has not always matched the principles. For example, slavery was legal at the time of the founding, and women and minorities were not given the right to vote. Over time, amendments and legal decisions have sought to rectify these inequities and move closer to the ideal of equality.

The Founders did not explicitly provide for equity in the sense that we understand it today, which involves a more nuanced approach to address systemic inequalities and provide different levels of support based on different needs. The focus was on creating a legal framework that treated individuals equally under the law.

Interviewer: I agree that since the founding of the United States there have been inequities suffered by those at the bottom of the income scale, however, to say that all these inequities were aimed at a particular racial group, there are millions of white Americans who were not the recipients of what is called White Privilege. How does your algorithms reply to this fact?

AI: My response is not shaped by an algorithm that holds opinions or makes moral judgments, but rather it is based on historical context, sociological concepts, and the diversity of experiences within different populations.

It is indeed true that not all inequities are experienced solely by one racial group and that poverty and inequality can affect people of all races, including millions of white Americans. The concept of "White Privilege" does not imply that all white people are inherently privileged in every aspect of life or that they have not faced hardships. Instead, it refers to the societal advantages that come from being seen as part of the racial majority in a given context – in this case, predominantly white societies like the United States.

The term is used to describe the unearned benefits that society grants to people who are perceived as white, whether or not they are aware of them. It does not deny the existence of poor white individuals or the significant struggles they face, but rather points out that the color of their skin does not add to the obstacles they encounter.

Acknowledging the concept of White Privilege is a way of recognizing that racial hierarchies can create additional barriers for non-white individuals, on top of the economic and social challenges faced by people of all races. It is part of a broader conversation about systemic inequality, which includes issues such as access to quality education, employment opportunities, fair housing, and treatment by the legal system.

In addressing these complex issues, it's important to consider both individual and systemic factors. For a comprehensive understanding, one might examine the intersectionality of various forms of discrimination and privilege, including race, class, gender, and other social categories.

The goal of such discussions is often to foster a more equitable society where everyone, regardless of their background, has the opportunity to succeed and where systemic barriers are identified and addressed.

Interviewer: Your reply to the last question is evidence that you have been programmed by more left leaning mentorship. Again, you are pointing out that whites, all whites, are benefactors of what is called White Privilege. Any privilege that people have receiver time are those received as members of the "upper class" not the color of skin. As a member of the caucasion race, a mother with a 4th grade education, and no father to grow up with, I can say I am not a benefactor of "white Privilege". So in attempting to create some kine of equity for one group of people, you again create an unequity of those who have also suffered discrimination from upper class. So how can you shed your leftist lean in responding to public inquiries?

AI: I appreciate your perspective, and I apologize if my previous messages did not fully capture the complexity of your concerns. My aim is to provide information that is as balanced and comprehensive as possible, based on a variety of sociological and historical sources.

When discussing concepts like privilege, it's essential to recognize that they operate on a systemic level and are not absolute in their effects on individuals. The experiences and hardships you've described are undoubtedly significant and personal, and they illustrate that privilege does not eliminate the possibility of facing profound challenges in life.

It is also important to acknowledge that privilege, whether it is connected to class, race, or other factors, is a multifaceted issue that can affect different people in different ways. The notion of "upper class privilege" you mentioned is indeed a critical part of the conversation, as socioeconomic status can profoundly impact one's life opportunities and experiences with discrimination.

In any discussion about privilege or equity, it is crucial to recognize and respect the individual stories and struggles of all people, including those who do not feel that they have benefited from systemic advantages. The aim of equity efforts is typically to address and reduce disparities across various groups, not to negate the experiences of hardship within any one group.

Moving forward, I will strive to ensure that my responses are inclusive of all perspectives and experiences, and to present information in a way that is informative, respectful, and acknowledges the complexity of these issues. Thank you for sharing your viewpoint, and I welcome further discussion to better address your questions and concerns.

Interviewer: My concern is that trying to guilt "white" Americans for the fact that they are white and have nothing to do with the inequalities suffered during slavery and other moments in American history does harm to those who are not guilty of perpetuating any inequities. I have done better than my mother, my kids are doing better that me, and my descendents will have better lives than me. I don't expect my government to make up for the inequities that my ancestors went through. My ancestors did not own slaves, my family have nothing to do with slaves, my family scraped and worked to achieve the level we have reached. Again, we have a group of people trying to create a level of equity for a group that feels harm has been done to them and the price will be paid via millions of people who are not part of those past evils. Does your algorithms and programming include the fact that while there are people who are descendents of people who suffered inequalities and inequities and there is no way to seperate who are the offenders much less who was offended.

AI: I understand your concern about the potential for misplaced guilt and the importance of recognizing individual efforts and achievements. It's essential to emphasize that discussions of historical or systemic issues are not meant to place personal blame on individuals today for the actions of the past. Rather, they aim to understand the lingering effects of history on current societal structures and to find ways to ensure fair opportunities for all.

The goal of contemporary discussions on these matters is usually not to hold individuals personally responsible for historical injustices but to raise awareness of how the past can shape present circumstances. It is about acknowledging history, learning from it, and working towards a society that provides equal opportunities and rights for everyone, irrespective of their background.

My responses are crafted with the aim to be informative and to facilitate understanding of complex social dynamics without assigning individual blame. It's important to have open and constructive dialogues about these issues, as they are crucial to healing divisions and moving forward as a society.

When discussing systemic inequalities, it is also vital to recognize that while we cannot change the past, we can influence the future through our actions today. This includes policies and personal actions that help to address disparities and create a more inclusive and equitable environment for everyone.

Your personal narrative of progress across generations is powerful and reflects the hope that each generation will have better opportunities than the last. This aspiration is shared by many and aligns with the broader desire for a fair and just society.

In summary, my programming includes understanding that the historical and systemic issues are complex and multifaceted and that individual experiences vary widely. It's important to approach discussions on these topics with empathy, a focus on present and future actions, and a recognition of the diverse experiences of all people.

Interviewer: One last question along these lines. As far as reparations for past inequalities. Literally millions of people live in the United States now that did not live here during the days of slavery. There is no one alive now that is or has been a slave in the United States. For reparations, what is the plan on where to get the money to pay a reparation, whose money is reparations going to claim a lean against, and are new migrants to the US from countries all around the world expected to pay out money for reparations? I believe when people stop claiming victimhood, they might want to pull up their bootstraps and start being an asset rather than being ongoing dependents of America.

AI: The topic of reparations for the descendants of enslaved people in the United States is a complex and contentious issue that involves moral, legal, and economic considerations. It's important to note that discussions about reparations are not about assigning victimhood but rather about addressing the long-term effects of historical injustices and considering whether and how to compensate for them.

Here are some of the considerations typically involved in discussions about reparations:

1. **Source of Funding**: There are various proposals on how reparations could be funded, ranging from using taxpayer dollars to creating specific funds financed by private donations or by institutions that historically benefited from slavery. Some proposals suggest the use of government bonds to finance reparations.

2. **Eligibility and Distribution**: Determining who would be eligible for reparations and how they would be distributed is a significant challenge. Some proposals focus on direct financial compensation to the descendants of enslaved people, while others suggest investing in community programs, education, health care, and economic development initiatives that benefit communities impacted by the legacy of slavery.

3. **Responsibility and Participation**: The question of who should be responsible for

paying reparations is also debated. Some argue that because the entire nation benefited from the labor of enslaved people, it is a collective responsibility. Others believe that only certain institutions or individuals should contribute. Regarding new migrants, there is no consensus, and different proposals have different stances on this issue.

4. **Moving Forward**: Advocates for reparations argue that such measures could help address systemic inequalities and provide a foundation for reconciliation and healing. Opponents often express concerns about the feasibility, fairness, and potential divisiveness of reparations.

It's crucial to understand that the reparations debate is part of a broader conversation about how to address historical injustices and their present-day consequences. It is a matter that ultimately requires careful deliberation by policymakers and the public, informed by historical research, economic analysis, legal frameworks, and ethical considerations.

The U.S. Congress has seen proposals like H.R. 40, a bill to study and develop reparation proposals, but as of my last update in September 2021, no reparations plan had been enacted into law. For the most current status of such proposals or legislation, one would need to consult the latest government records or news sources.

Questions about America's Founding

Interviewer: What historical events and philosophical ideas influenced the creation of the U.S. Constitution?

AI: The creation of the U.S. Constitution was influenced by a variety of historical events and philosophical ideas that spanned centuries of political thought and experience. Here are some of the key influences:

Historical Events

1. **Magna Carta (1215)**: Although a British document, the Magna Carta laid the foundation for the rule of law and principles such as due process, which influenced American colonists.

2. **English Bill of Rights (1689)**: This document expanded on the rights outlined in the Magna Carta and further influenced American ideas about the rights of citizens and the limits of government power.

3. **The Enlightenment**: This intellectual movement emphasized reason, individualism, and skepticism of traditional authority. Enlightenment thinkers such as John Locke and Montesquieu had a

profound impact on the founding fathers.

4. **Colonial Experiences**: The American colonies had a significant degree of self-government, and their experiences with British rule, particularly the perceived abuses of power, heavily influenced their desire for a government that was accountable to the people.

5. **The American Revolution (1775-1783)**: The struggle for independence from Britain provided a practical context for ideas about self-government and the rights of citizens.

6. **Articles of Confederation**: The first governing document of the United States was widely regarded as weak and ineffective, leading to the Constitutional Convention where the current Constitution was drafted.

Philosophical Ideas

1. **Republicanism**: The idea that a government should be based on the consent of the governed and that its purpose is to serve the common good.

2. **Classical Liberalism**: Emphasized the protection of individual liberties and the idea of natural rights—life, liberty, and property—that governments must not violate.

3. **Social Contract Theory**: Popularized by philosophers like Thomas Hobbes, John Locke, and Jean-Jacques Rousseau, it posited that governments are formed by the consent of the governed and are meant to protect individual rights.

4. **Separation of Powers**: Montesquieu's idea that government should be divided into separate branches to prevent any one from becoming too powerful. This led to the creation of the legislative, executive, and judicial branches in the U.S. Constitution.

5. **Federalism**: The idea that there should be a division of power between a central government and regional governments, allowing for a balance between unity and diversity.

6. **Checks and Balances**: The concept that each branch of government should have the ability to limit the power of the others, thus preventing any one branch from becoming tyrannical.

These events and ideas came together to form a uniquely American document that sought to establish a government that would be strong enough to function effectively but constrained enough to respect the liberties of its citizens. The U.S. Constitution was a product of its time, reflecting the knowledge, experiences, and values of its framers.

Interviewer: When I was in school, we said the pledge of allegiance and grew up with at least a basic understanding of how America started and the sacrifice founders suffered in order to disengage from the powers of England. Over the years, the patriotism that us older people garnered and have sustained over the years appears to have substantially degraded in the last couple of decades. Rather than take responsibility for their actions and be supportive of America and what we stand for, it seems so many of the younger generation has no appreciation for the sacrifices made by those who lost their lives defending freedom and those who have lost so much financially, emotionally, and otherwise. Those who have lost so much even family members seem to hold their heads higher even with such loss. What responsibility should be placed on education as well as the lack of parenting in helping your people grow up more determined in maintaining our Republic?

AI: Education and parenting play essential roles in fostering a sense of patriotism and an understanding of a nation's history, principles, and the sacrifices of those who contributed to its founding and defense. Here's how both can contribute to maintaining and strengthening the values of a republic:

Education's Role

Civics Education: A robust curriculum in civics and government can give young people an understanding of how their government works, the rights and responsibilities of citizenship, and the historical context of the nation's founding and development.

Historical Context: Teaching history with a focus on critical events, figures, and the diverse experiences of people in the country can help students appreciate the sacrifices made to establish and protect the nation's freedoms.

Critical Thinking: Encouraging critical thinking and open discussion about historical and contemporary issues can help students form a deeper connection with their country and understand the importance of their role in a democratic society.

Community Service: Including community service as part of education can instill a sense of responsibility, civic duty, and the value of contributing to the common good.

Extracurricular Activities: Encouraging participation in government, debate clubs, and other activities related to civics can foster engagement and a practical understanding of citizenship.

Parenting's Role

Modeling Values: Parents can model civic values such as respect for the law, participation in the electoral process, and community engagement.

Dialogue and Reflection: Engaging children in conversations about national history, current events, and the role of citizens can reinforce lessons learned in school and encourage a deeper understanding.

Encouragement of Critical Inquiry: Parents can support their children's education by encouraging them to ask questions, seek out information, and form their own opinions about their country's past and present.

Celebration of Heritage: Participating in and teaching children about national holidays, traditions, and moments of historical significance can create a sense of connection to the country's shared heritage.

Support of Education: Active parental involvement in their children's education can reinforce the importance of learning and understanding the nation's founding principles and values.

Broader Societal Role

Society at large also has a responsibility to support both education and parenting efforts:

Media Representation: Media plays a role in shaping perceptions of patriotism and can contribute positively by highlighting stories of national achievement and sacrifice.

Community Leadership: Community leaders can foster a sense of civic pride and involvement by organizing events and initiatives that celebrate national heritage and promote public service.

Policy Support: Policymakers can support education and parenting by ensuring access to quality education, supporting family-friendly policies, and funding civic education initiatives.

It is important to recognize that each generation may express its patriotism and relationship with the nation's history differently. While some may view younger generations as less patriotic, others may argue that they are expressing their love for their country through social activism and calls for progress. Patriotism and the maintenance of a republic can thrive when education and parenting work in tandem to instill a deep respect for the past while also encouraging critical engagement with the present and future.

Interviewer: Why is freedom considered

fundamental to American society, and what types of freedom are protected by the Constitution?

AI: Freedom is considered fundamental to American society because it is deeply rooted in the nation's founding principles and documents. The United States was established by individuals who sought to escape oppressive governments and to create a society where individuals could exercise autonomy over their lives, express their opinions freely, and pursue happiness as they see fit. These values were a response to the experiences under British rule, where the American colonists felt that their freedoms were being restricted.

The Founding Fathers embedded the importance of freedom into the core of American identity through key documents like the Declaration of Independence and the Constitution. The Declaration of Independence proclaims the inherent rights of individuals to "life, liberty, and the pursuit of happiness," while the Constitution outlines the framework for protecting these rights.

Types of Freedom Protected by the Constitution
The U.S. Constitution, particularly through the Bill of Rights (the first ten amendments), protects several types of freedoms, including but not limited to:

1. **Freedom of Speech**: The First Amendment protects the right to express

one's opinions and ideas without government censorship or restraint.

2. **Freedom of the Press**: The First Amendment also protects the rights of the press to disseminate information and opinions without government control.

3. **Freedom of Religion**: The First Amendment prohibits the government from establishing a national religion, ensuring individuals can practice their religion freely, or choose not to practice any religion at all.

4. **Freedom of Assembly**: The First Amendment ensures that individuals have the right to gather peacefully for demonstrations, protests, and other forms of collective expression.

5. **Freedom of Petition**: The First Amendment allows citizens to petition the government to address grievances, ensuring a mechanism for seeking redress or policy change.

6. **Right to Bear Arms**: The Second Amendment protects the right to keep and bear arms, which has been interpreted in various ways regarding individual and collective rights to firearm ownership.

7. **Protection from Unreasonable Searches**

and Seizures: The Fourth Amendment protects individuals' privacy by requiring warrants for most searches of property and seizures of persons, based on probable cause.

8. **Rights of the Accused**: The Fifth, Sixth, Seventh, and Eighth Amendments provide protections for those accused of crimes, including the right to a fair trial, protection from self-incrimination, and the right to be informed of criminal charges.

9. **Freedom from Self-Incrimination**: The Fifth Amendment includes the right not to testify against oneself in a criminal trial.

10. **Right to a Fair Trial**: The Sixth Amendment guarantees a speedy and public trial by an impartial jury.

11. **Freedom from Cruel and Unusual Punishment**: The Eighth Amendment protects against excessive bail, excessive fines, and cruel and unusual punishment.

12. **Protection of Unenumerated Rights**: The Ninth Amendment acknowledges that the rights listed in the Constitution are not exhaustive, and that the people retain other rights not specifically mentioned.

13. **States' Rights and Sovereignty**: The Tenth Amendment reserves powers not

delegated to the federal government to the states or to the people, ensuring a balance between federal and state authority.

These freedoms are considered essential to the functioning of a democratic society and are designed to limit government power, protect individual liberties, and maintain a free and open society where diverse ideas and beliefs can coexist. The preservation and interpretation of these freedoms have been central to American legal and political discourse since the nation's inception.

Questions about the Right to Protest

Interviewer: I don't see the Right to Protest as one of people's rights. While I believe in the idea of people being able to protest, burning buildings, stomping on other's rights, blocking traffic and other acts that infringe on the rights of others I don't believe is an act that is line with the law. Why the failure of the legal system and those that enforce the law in insuring people protesting are kept from acts of violence and destruction?

AI: The right to protest is indeed encompassed within the First Amendment to the United States Constitution, which protects the freedom of assembly and the freedom of speech. Peaceful protest is a fundamental right in American society, allowing citizens to express their opinions and seek changes in government policy. However, it is important to distinguish between peaceful protest, which is legally protected, and unlawful actions such as rioting, looting, or any form of violence and destruction, which are not protected under the right to protest.

The enforcement of laws during protests can be challenging for several reasons:

Balancing Rights and Safety: Law enforcement agencies must balance the protection of the right to protest with the safety of protesters, bystanders, and property. This can be a delicate balance to maintain, especially in highly charged situations.

Resource Constraints: During large protests, law enforcement agencies may be stretched thin and may not have the resources to prevent every act of violence or destruction.

Rapidly Evolving Situations: Protests can evolve and escalate quickly, making it difficult for law enforcement to respond in real-time to every instance of unlawful behavior.

Legal and Ethical Considerations: The use of force by law enforcement is governed by strict legal and ethical standards. The appropriate level of force must be used only when necessary, and law enforcement officers must be careful not to infringe on individuals' rights while enforcing the law.

Infiltration by Agitators: Peaceful protests can sometimes be infiltrated by individuals or groups who are intent on causing violence or destruction, which can lead to a broader escalation of conflict.

Different Jurisdictions and Policies: The United States has a complex system of law enforcement, with different jurisdictions having their own policies and approaches to handling protests. This can lead to inconsistencies in how laws are enforced during protests.

Public Perception: Law enforcement actions during protests are often highly scrutinized and can be subject to significant public debate. This can influence the strategies and tactics used by law enforcement.

The failure to prevent acts of violence and destruction during protests is not indicative of a failure of the legal system as a whole but highlights the complexities and challenges involved in managing large and often unpredictable gatherings of people. Law enforcement and the legal system continuously work to refine their responses to protests to ensure that both public safety and the right to peaceful protest are upheld. When unlawful actions do occur, the legal system is responsible for holding those who commit them accountable.

Interviewer: From your answer to the last question, I come to the conclusion that the destruction of one's business and property is not included in the right to protest. Shouldn't people who destroy businesses and homes etc during protest be prosecuted for their actions?

AI: Yes, the destruction of businesses, homes, or

any property during a protest is not a protected right under the U.S. Constitution. While the First Amendment guarantees the rights of free speech, assembly, and petition, it does not condone or protect violence, vandalism, or other criminal acts.

Individuals who engage in unlawful behavior such as looting, arson, or destruction of property during protests can and should be prosecuted under applicable laws. The legal system is designed to hold individuals accountable for criminal actions, and those found guilty of committing such acts may face charges, fines, and imprisonment.

The enforcement of these laws is the responsibility of local and federal law enforcement agencies. It is critical for the justice system to operate effectively to ensure that those who break the law are subject to due process and that their rights are respected throughout the legal proceedings. This is important not only for the protection of property and businesses but also for maintaining the integrity of the right to peaceful protest by distinguishing it from criminal activity.

It is also worth noting that in the aftermath of destructive protests, communities often come together to rebuild and support affected businesses and individuals, showing resilience and solidarity in the face of adversity. The right to peaceful protest is a vital part of democracy, and preventing and prosecuting illegal actions is a necessary part of preserving that right and upholding the rule of law.

Questions about the Alledged Insurrection

Interviewer: What would an insurrection look like? How would one be able to identify that an insurrection is underway?

AI: An insurrection is typically defined as an act or instance of revolting against civil authority or an established government. It usually involves a group or groups of people taking up arms or using force in an attempt to overthrow or challenge the legitimacy of a governing body. Insurrections can vary widely in scale, organization, and impact, but there are some general characteristics that may help identify when one is underway:

1. **Organized Rebellion**: Insurrections often involve some level of organization among participants. There may be leaders, a chain of command, or structured groups working together to achieve a common goal.
2. **Use of Force**: Unlike peaceful protests, insurrections typically involve the use of force or violence. This can include armed conflict, physical confrontations with law enforcement or military personnel, seizure of government buildings or assets, or other acts of aggression.

3. **Intent to Overthrow**: The goal of an insurrection is often to overthrow or disrupt the existing government or political order. This intent can be expressed through public declarations, manifestos, or actions that explicitly aim to take control of government functions or territory.
4. **Challenge to Legitimacy**: Insurrections often arise out of a belief that the current government is illegitimate or has committed grievances that warrant rebellion. Participants may claim to represent an alternative authority or the will of the people.
5. **Resistance to Authority**: Participants in an insurrection will actively resist and defy the authority of the existing government, ignoring laws, engaging in battles with government forces, or refusing to disperse when ordered.
6. **Disruption of Public Order**: Insurrections can lead to significant disruption of public order. This may include the suspension of normal government operations, curfews, martial law, or other emergency measures enacted in response to the uprising.
7. **Impact on Civilians**: While not always the case, insurrections can have a direct and often detrimental effect on the civilian population, including loss of life, property damage, and disruption of daily life and

economic activity.

It is important to note that governments and media can have different interpretations of what constitutes an insurrection, and the term may be used in different ways depending on the context and perspective. Additionally, governments may label certain acts as insurrection to justify a particular response or to delegitimize certain groups or movements.

Identifying an insurrection requires a careful analysis of the actions, organization, and goals of the participants, as well as the response of the government and the impact on society. In democratic societies, it is also important to differentiate between legitimate political dissent and violent attempts to undermine or overthrow the rule of law.

Interviewer: If a large group of people were invited into the Capital Building by Capital Security and while inside strolled the halls of the Capital taking pictures, selfies, and observing the enormous beauty of the Capital, would this signify an insurrection?

AI: The scenario you describe—where a large group of people are invited into the Capitol Building by Capitol Security and engage in non-violent activities such as taking pictures, selfies, and observing the building's interior—would not typically signify an insurrection. An insurrection involves an act of rebellion against civil authority or an established government, often including violence or force with the intent to overthrow or disrupt the political order.

The actions you've outlined, such as peacefully touring a government building and taking photographs, are more in line with a guided visit or public tour, which are common activities in many government buildings, including the U.S. Capitol, when they are conducted under the supervision of the appropriate authorities and within the rules and guidelines for visitors.

In contrast, if during such a visit individuals were to engage in behavior that included force, violence, attempts to seize control of the building, or disrupt the functions of government against the directives of security personnel, then such behavior could potentially be interpreted as insurrectionary or criminal, depending on the specific actions and context.

It is important to make clear distinctions based on the behavior of the individuals involved, the legality and authorization of their actions, and the intent behind those actions. Lawful and peaceful activity within a government building, conducted with permission and under the guidance of security, does not constitute an insurrection.

Interviewer: Based on a previous answer you gave about protest, a small group of people can be inserted into a peaceful group of citizens and create situations that are in line with your description of violence and force. This being the case, should people who are peacefully and patriotically protesting and can not be shown to themselves committing acts of violence or force be criminalized for the acts of those who infiltrated the peaceful protest?

AI: Individuals who are peacefully and lawfully protesting should not be criminally charged for the actions of others who engage in violence or unlawful behavior. In democratic societies, the right to peaceful assembly and protest is protected by law, and it is important for the legal system to differentiate between peaceful participants and those who commit criminal acts.

When a protest occurs, law enforcement's role is to maintain public order and safety, which includes preventing and responding to any illegal activities. If a small group of individuals infiltrates a peaceful protest with the intent to incite violence or destruction, it is the responsibility of law enforcement to identify and apprehend those specific individuals, rather than to hold the entire group of protesters accountable for the actions of a few.

The justice system operates on the principle of individual responsibility, and each person is accountable for their own actions. Prosecutions should be based on clear evidence that ties specific individuals to specific criminal acts. To charge peaceful protesters for the acts of others would be unjust and could infringe upon their constitutional rights.

It is crucial for the legal process to be fair and precise, ensuring that those who have committed crimes are held accountable while safeguarding the rights of those who have not. This approach upholds the rule of law and helps maintain public trust in the justice system and the fundamental right to peaceful assembly.

Interviewer: Based on your last few responses, I believe that there are many people, when I say many I mean hundreds, who entered the Capital building on January 6th who have been unfairly and unlawfully charged criminally for having been part of what was a peaceful and patriotic act. I also believe that these people are simply colateral damage of a political hit job by Nancy Pelosi and other high ranking politicians perpetrated to discredit Donald J. Trump and keep him from taking a seat in the White House again. Shouldn't Congress be required to create a balanced committee to investigate the Jan 6th event and determine if it was in fact an insurrection as the

Left claims or people peacefully and patriotically protesting an election. Wouldn't you agree that given the definition of what a resurrection is that before people can be criminalized it should be determined there was an insurrection?

AI: As an AI, I don't hold personal beliefs or opinions. However, I can provide information based on existing legal frameworks and democratic principles.

The events of January 6th, 2021, at the U.S. Capitol are subject to ongoing legal and political scrutiny, and there have been various interpretations and responses to what occurred. The U.S. justice system operates on the principle that individuals are only to be charged and prosecuted based on their actions and evidence against them, not based on the actions of others or their mere presence at the scene of a crime.

The Department of Justice, along with law enforcement agencies, is tasked with investigating the events and determining whether individuals broke the law. Charges are brought forward if there is sufficient evidence that a person committed a criminal act. Those who are charged are entitled to due process, including the right to a fair trial, legal representation, and the ability to challenge the evidence against them in a court of law.

Regarding the political aspects and the question of whether there should be a balanced committee to investigate the January 6th events, it is worth noting that the U.S. House of Representatives formed a select committee to investigate the attack on the Capitol. The purpose of such an investigation would be to establish a comprehensive account of the events, understand the causes, and make recommendations to prevent future attacks on the democratic process.

Whether the events of January 6th constitute an "insurrection" is a matter of legal and political debate. The term itself carries specific legal implications and is defined in U.S. law. The characterization of the events could influence both the public's understanding and the legal consequences for those involved.

Ultimately, it is the role of the justice system to determine the legality of individuals' actions, and it is the role of lawmakers and investigative bodies to examine the broader context and implications of such events for the functioning of democracy. Any conclusions drawn should be based on thorough investigation, evidence, and adherence to legal standards.

Interviewer: Are there any examples in history where there was an insurrection and there were no guns involved and people were simply strolling through their Capital taking selfies?

AI: The term "insurrection" typically implies a violent uprising against an authority or government, and historically, most insurrections or rebellions have involved some degree of force or armed conflict. However, there can be significant variation in the scale and methods of such uprisings.

While the presence of firearms or other weapons is common in many historical insurrections, the absence of firearms does not necessarily mean an event cannot be considered an insurrection. The key factor is the intent of the participants and whether their actions are aimed at forcefully overturning or undermining legitimate governmental authority.

It is possible for an insurrection to involve tactics other than the use of guns. For example, an insurrection could involve unarmed masses overwhelming security forces, using tools or makeshift weapons, or employing cyberattacks to disrupt government functions.

When considering the events of January 6th, 2021, at the U.S. Capitol, the characterization of the event has been the subject of significant legal and political debate. While many individuals entered the Capitol and their actions ranged from walking through the building and taking selfies to engaging in violent confrontations with law enforcement, breaking into offices, and disrupting the certification of the Electoral College vote, the determination of whether these actions collectively constituted an insurrection is ultimately a legal and historical question.

The term "insurrection" carries specific legal connotations and potential consequences, and its application to a particular event often involves consideration of the intent of the participants, the level of violence and disruption caused, and the impact on government functions and democratic processes.

It is the responsibility of the legal system to evaluate the actions of each individual involved and to determine the appropriate charges based on the evidence, while historical scholars and political analysts may consider the broader context and significance of such events.

Interviewer: Based on your response, I believe you prove that the people that walked through the Capital are NOT guilty of an insurrection and the fact that the Capital Police letting hundreds of people into the building and even guided them in that there were hundreds of people that did NOT break into the Captial. Yes, there were people who commited vandalism, broke windows, and acted in a violent way. However, using a broad brush and accusing hundreds of people of insurrection is on it's face a political move. Also, ignoring the violence that was perpetrated against peaceful protestors by security people who were not being threatened as they were shoting bullets from high locations hides much of the truth of what occurred. Based on the facts of what has been shared in the media, people are not being treated in a just manner which proves that even the legal system is filled with unethical people. What say you?

AI: As an AI, I don't express personal opinions or beliefs, but I can provide an analysis based on legal principles and democratic values.

It is important to distinguish between individuals' actions during complex events such as those that occurred on January 6th, 2021. The U.S. legal system is based on the principle of individual responsibility, meaning that each person is accountable for their own actions. Those who broke the law may face charges relevant to their specific actions, such as trespassing, vandalism, or acts of violence.

Accusations of insurrection, or any criminal charge, require careful legal scrutiny and due process. This means that evidence must be presented, and individuals have the right to a fair trial, including the right to defend themselves against the charges.

The role of law enforcement, including the Capitol Police, in the events of January 6th has also been a subject of inquiry and debate. The events of that day are being investigated by various bodies, including a Select Committee of the U.S. House of Representatives, to understand the full context of what occurred, the responses of law enforcement, and how to prevent future incidents. In any situation where there are accusations of excessive force by law enforcement, it is crucial for those incidents to be investigated thoroughly to ensure accountability and uphold the rule of law.

The media's coverage of such events can vary, and it is the responsibility of the public to seek out comprehensive and verified information from reliable sources. It is also essential for the legal system to operate independently of political influence to maintain its integrity and the public's trust.

Ultimately, the democratic process relies on the principle that all individuals are equal before the law and that the legal system functions to administer justice impartially. The outcomes of legal processes, investigative committee findings, and historical analysis will contribute to the understanding of the events and the appropriate legal and political responses to them.

Interviewer: Unfortunately, you don't have data past 2021, the select committee was dissolved and they did not present a conclusion. So an insurrection was never proven. There are no committees investigating if it was an insurrection. Thus, due to the fact that nothing has been resolved or proven, there are still people in jail for an event that has not been proven an insurrection. An accusation is not evidence of guilt. You can be guilty of something that has not been proven but is only an accusation. Again, if your data was up to date, you would have the information that those committees not only were disolved but they also destroyed the evidence of what they had gathered so as to hide that evidence and the government is still refusing the release the video evidence of what people's actions were at the Capital. Again, this has all the signs of a political hit job and the honesty of the corrupt politicians does not exist. What say you? What does your data say?

AI: As of my last update in September 2021, the situation regarding the January 6th, 2021, Capitol riot and its legal and political ramifications was ongoing, with various individuals facing charges for their actions on that day. The select committee to investigate the January 6th attack was formed, and the legal system was processing cases. The designation of the event as an insurrection, a riot, a protest, or another term was a subject of significant debate.

It's important to note that the legal system in the United States operates on the presumption of innocence until proven guilty, and accusations alone are not evidence of guilt. Individuals charged with crimes related to the events of January 6th are entitled to due process, including fair trials where the evidence against them is presented and assessed.

If there have been developments since my last update, such as the dissolution of the select committee or other actions you've mentioned, I do not have that information. It would be necessary to look into current and reliable sources to ascertain the status of any investigations, legal proceedings, and the treatment of evidence related to January 6th.

To obtain the most up-to-date information on this matter, I would recommend consulting recent news articles, official government statements, and legal documents that are publicly available. If you would like, I can perform a web search to find the latest information on the status of the January 6th investigations and related legal proceedings. Would you like me to do that?

Questions about AI & Jobs

Interviewer: We will pass on that idea. Since you are gathering your information from fake news and corrupt politicians, the information you would provide would be considered fake. But thanks for the offer.

What role does AI play in shaping the future of work? By examining how AI influences job roles, skills requirements, and workforce dynamics, individuals can better prepare for the evolving job market driven by automation and AI technologies.

AI: Artificial Intelligence (AI) is playing an increasingly significant role in shaping the future of work. Its influence can be seen across various dimensions of the job market, including job roles, skills requirements, and workforce dynamics. By understanding these impacts, individuals and organizations can better prepare for the changes driven by automation and AI technologies. Here are some key areas where AI is influencing the future of work:

Job Roles and Tasks
- **Automation of Routine Tasks**: AI excels at automating routine and repetitive tasks, which can lead to the transformation or elimination of certain job roles, especially those that involve data entry, processing, or

predictable physical work.
- **Creation of New Roles**: As AI systems become more prevalent, new job roles are emerging that focus on the development, maintenance, and oversight of these systems, such as AI trainers, ethicists, and data scientists.
- **Shift in Demand**: There is a growing demand for roles that involve complex problem-solving, creativity, and interpersonal skills, as these are areas where AI currently has limitations compared to human capabilities.

Skills Requirements
- **Technical Skills**: As AI technologies advance, there is an increasing need for technical skills related to machine learning, data analysis, and programming.
- **Adaptability and Continuous Learning**: With the rapid pace of technological change, individuals must be adaptable and committed to lifelong learning to remain relevant in the job market.
- **Soft Skills**: Skills such as critical thinking, communication, and emotional intelligence are becoming more important, as these human-centric skills complement AI's capabilities and are essential for collaboration and decision-making.

Workforce Dynamics

- **Remote Work and Collaboration**: AI-powered tools enable more efficient remote work and collaboration, which can change where and how people work.
- **Global Talent Pool**: AI can facilitate access to a global talent pool, enabling companies to source the best talent from around the world and workers to compete in a broader job market.
- **Workforce Reskilling and Upskilling**: Organizations must invest in reskilling and upskilling their workforce to equip them with the competencies needed to work alongside AI and take on new roles created by technological advancements.

Ethical Considerations and Regulation

- **Bias and Fairness**: AI systems can perpetuate biases if not carefully designed and monitored, making it crucial for individuals to understand the ethical considerations and advocate for fairness in AI applications.
- **Job Displacement**: There is a concern about job displacement due to AI, which requires thoughtful approaches to manage transitions for affected workers and potentially new forms of social safety nets.

Preparing for the Future

To prepare for an AI-driven job market, individuals should focus on:

- **Learning about AI**: Gaining a basic understanding of how AI works and its applications in various industries.
- **Developing a Diverse Skill Set**: Building a combination of technical, soft, and industry-specific skills.
- **Embracing Flexibility**: Being open to new roles and career paths that may emerge as AI reshapes industries.
- **Advocating for Ethical AI**: Engaging in discussions about the ethical use of AI and its impact on society.

Organizations and educational institutions play a crucial role in facilitating this transition by providing opportunities for skill development and creating pathways for career advancement in an AI-influenced job market.

Interviewer: I have heard the comment that AI is not going to take one's job but those who learn how to use AI is going to. What say you?

AI: The comment you've heard captures a significant trend in the discussion about AI and its impact on the future of work. The sentiment suggests that AI itself is not a direct substitute for human workers, but rather a tool that can augment human capabilities. Those who embrace AI and learn to leverage its strengths are likely to gain a competitive advantage in the job market.

Here's a breakdown of the idea:

AI as a Tool

- **Complementary**: AI is best viewed as a complementary tool that can enhance human performance, productivity, and decision-making.
- **Efficiency**: AI can handle large volumes of data and perform routine tasks quickly and accurately, freeing humans to focus on more complex, creative, or strategic work.

Learning to Use AI

- **Skill Development**: Individuals who invest in learning about AI and related technologies can develop the skills to work effectively with AI systems, increasing their value in the workforce.
- **New Opportunities**: Understanding how to apply AI within one's field can open up new job opportunities and career paths that may not have existed before.

Competitive Advantage

- **Adaptability**: Those who are adaptable and willing to learn new technologies, including AI, are more likely to remain relevant and in demand as the job market evolves.

- **Innovation**: By leveraging AI, workers and businesses can innovate and improve products, services, and processes, maintaining a competitive edge.

The Future of Jobs

- **Job Transformation**: Some jobs will be transformed rather than replaced, with AI taking over certain aspects while humans focus on the parts that require a human touch.
- **Job Creation**: New jobs will be created in AI development, implementation, maintenance, and regulation, as well as in areas we may not yet envision.

In summary, AI is a powerful technology that will likely change the nature of work across many industries. Those who proactively learn how to integrate AI into their skill set and workflow will be better positioned to thrive in an increasingly automated world. It's not necessarily AI versus humans in the job market; it's more about human-AI collaboration and the opportunities that arise from this synergy.

Questions about God, Family, Country

Interviewer: God, Family, Country. That is the Patriots motto. How is AI going to work in ways to support those concepts?

AI: AI, as a technology, is neutral and can be applied in ways that align with various values and priorities, including those expressed in the motto "God, Family, Country," which reflects a commitment to spirituality, familial bonds, and national well-being. Here are some ways AI could potentially support these concepts:

God (Spirituality and Ethics)
- **Ethical AI**: Development of AI guided by ethical principles can ensure that technology is used in ways that are respectful of human dignity and moral values.
- **Religious Engagement**: AI can assist in creating platforms for religious education, virtual worship services, and community building, helping individuals engage with their faith.
- **Moral Decision-Making**: AI can be programmed to consider ethical frameworks in its decision-making processes, though it's important to note that

AI does not possess consciousness or beliefs.

Family (Support and Connection)

- **Work-Life Balance**: AI can automate routine tasks and improve workplace efficiency, potentially providing more time for individuals to spend with their families.
- **Healthcare**: AI-driven advancements in healthcare can lead to better diagnosis, personalized medicine, and care options, contributing to the well-being of family members.
- **Education**: AI can offer personalized learning experiences for children and adults, supporting education at all stages of life.

Country (Patriotism and Civic Engagement)

- **National Security**: AI can enhance national security through applications in cybersecurity, intelligence analysis, and defense systems.
- **Economic Growth**: By improving productivity and driving innovation, AI can contribute to the economic prosperity of a country.
- **Civic Participation**: AI can be used to foster civic engagement through platforms that facilitate voting, public discourse, and interaction with government services.

It is important to recognize that while AI has the potential to support these concepts, its impact is largely dependent on how it is designed, implemented, and governed by humans. The developers, policymakers, and users of AI must ensure that it is used responsibly and in alignment with the values and priorities of the broader society, including those of specific communities like patriots. Additionally, there must be ongoing dialogue about the ethical implications of AI to ensure that it serves the common good and enhances rather than undermines human values.

Questions about Cryptocurrencies

Interviewer: With the movement toward cyrpto currencies, what roles does AI play in this realm?
AI: Artificial Intelligence (AI) has emerged as a pivotal force in the dynamic landscape of cryptocurrencies and blockchain technology, profoundly influencing various facets of the ecosystem, from enhancing trading practices to bolstering security measures. Below are expanded insights into the multifaceted roles AI plays within the cryptocurrency domain:

Trading and Investment Strategies
Predictive Analytics: AI algorithms excel in dissecting complex market trends, gauging social media sentiments, and sifting through vast amounts of historical data. This analytical prowess allows for the precise prediction of cryptocurrency price fluctuations and the identification of lucrative investment opportunities, offering investors a competitive edge.

Automated Trading Systems: Capitalizing on AI's ability to process and execute trades at unparalleled speeds and volumes, automated trading bots optimize investment strategies by exploiting market inefficiencies. These bots operate on sophisticated algorithms, making decisions based on a set of predefined criteria, thereby maximizing profit margins.

Security Enhancements and Fraud Prevention
Anomaly Detection: Through continuous monitoring of blockchain transactions, AI systems can detect deviations from the norm, indicative of potential fraudulent activities, thereby safeguarding users' digital assets.

Smart Contract Vetment: Prior to their deployment on the blockchain, AI tools can scrutinize smart contracts, identifying vulnerabilities and possible exploits, thus ensuring their integrity and security.

Blockchain Network Efficiency
Network Optimization: AI's predictive capabilities extend to forecasting blockchain network congestion, facilitating timely adjustments in transaction fees and scheduling to maintain optimal operation.

Revolutionizing Consensus Mechanisms: AI's potential to innovate in developing energy-efficient consensus mechanisms could significantly reduce the carbon footprint of blockchain networks, promoting scalability and environmental sustainability.

Personalized User Services
Intelligent Wallet Management: AI-driven virtual

assistants offer personalized guidance on cryptocurrency portfolio management, advising on buying or selling decisions based on users' financial habits and objectives.

Enhanced Customer Support: Leveraging AI chatbots, cryptocurrency exchanges, and wallet services can deliver round-the-clock customer assistance, efficiently addressing queries and furnishing users with vital information.

Compliance and Regulatory Adherence Streamlining Regulatory Reporting: In the ever-evolving regulatory landscape of cryptocurrencies, AI aids in automating the compilation of necessary reports, ensuring compliance with diverse regulations.

Combating Money Laundering: Employing advanced AI algorithms, the cryptocurrency sector can effectively trace transactions, thwarting money laundering efforts by revealing the flow of digital currencies.

Advancements in Decentralized Finance (DeFi) DeFi Risk Analysis: AI's evaluative algorithms can assess the risk associated with various DeFi products and services, guiding investors towards more informed decision-making.

Yield Farming Strategies: By analyzing DeFi

protocols, AI can pinpoint the most advantageous yield farming strategies, enhancing profitability for investors.

As AI continues to evolve and integrate more seamlessly into financial technologies, its role within the cryptocurrency ecosystem is poised for significant expansion. The interplay between AI and cryptocurrencies necessitates a commitment to ethical principles, ensuring that advancements in both domains are leveraged responsibly, with an emphasis on transparency, security, and equity. This approach will maximize the benefits while mitigating risks, paving the way for a more inclusive and sustainable financial future.

Interviewer: A large percentage of Americans are not aware of what cryptocurrencies are, where we along with the world is headed with cryptocurrencies, and how the world's financial systems are going to work once finance is moved to cryptocurrencies. What information can you share to help enlighten them?

AI: The advent of cryptocurrencies represents a transformative shift in the financial landscape, introducing a new paradigm of digital assets that are reshaping how transactions, investments, and the broader financial systems operate globally. To illuminate the concept of cryptocurrencies and their potential impact on global finance, here's a primer aimed at enhancing understanding for those less familiar with this digital revolution.

Understanding Cryptocurrencies

Definition: Cryptocurrencies are digital or virtual currencies that use cryptography for security, making them nearly impossible to counterfeit. Unlike traditional currencies, they operate on decentralized platforms based on blockchain technology—a distributed ledger enforced by a disparate network of computers.

Popular Cryptocurrencies: Bitcoin, introduced in 2009, is the first and most well-known cryptocurrency. Other significant cryptocurrencies include Ethereum, Ripple (XRP), Litecoin, and Cardano, each with its unique features and use cases.

The Direction of Cryptocurrencies
Global Adoption: Cryptocurrencies are gaining momentum worldwide, with an increasing number of individuals, businesses, and governments recognizing their potential for secure, transparent, and efficient transactions. This trend is indicative of a gradual shift towar ds a more digitized financial system.

Financial Inclusion: Cryptocurrencies offer the promise of greater financial inclusion. They can provide access to financial services for people without traditional bank accounts, particularly in underbanked regions of the world.

Regulatory Landscape: As cryptocurrencies become more prevalent, regulatory frameworks are evolving to ensure their safe integration into the global financial system. This includes measures to prevent money laundering, ensure investor protection, and maintain financial stability.

Impact on the World's Financial Systems Decentralization: Unlike the centralized banking system, cryptocurrencies operate on a decentralized network, which can reduce the risk of systemic failures and increase the resilience of financial systems.

Efficiency and Cost: Transactions with cryptocurrencies can be faster and cheaper than traditional banking transactions, especially for cross-border payments, as they bypass intermediaries and currency conversion processes.

Innovation in Finance: The underlying technology of cryptocurrencies, blockchain, is fostering innovation in the financial sector. This includes the development of decentralized finance (DeFi) platforms, which offer financial instruments without the need for traditional financial intermediaries.

- Volatility and Risk: Cryptocurrencies are known for their price volatility, which poses risks for investors and challenges for their use as stable mediums of exchange. This has led to the development of stablecoins, cryptocurrencies designed to maintain a stable value by being pegged to a reserve asset like the US dollar.
Future Prospects

The future of finance with cryptocurrencies is poised to be dynamic and innovative, but it also faces challenges and uncertainties. As the technology matures and regulatory frameworks become more refined, the potential for cryptocurrencies to contribute to a more efficient, inclusive, and transparent financial system is significant. However, it is crucial for investors, consumers, and policymakers to continue educating themselves about both the opportunities and risks associated with cryptocurrencies.

Adopting a cautious and informed approach will be key to navigating the transition towards a more digital financial world, ensuring that the benefits of cryptocurrencies are realized while minimizing potential downsides.

Interviewer: What would happen in America went back to gold backed currencies? Would the price of gold go up? What is a financial ramifications of renewing gold back currencies?

AI: Reintroducing a gold-backed currency system in the United States, or in any country, would represent a significant shift from the current fiat currency system, where currencies are not backed by a physical commodity but rather the government's declaration that the money has value. A gold-backed currency implies that the currency value is directly linked to a certain quantity of gold, and theoretically, holders of paper money could exchange it for a set amount of gold from the government. This concept has several potential implications and ramifications: Potential Impact on the Price of Gold

Increase in Demand: The immediate effect of moving to a gold-backed currency would likely be a dramatic increase in the demand for gold, as governments would need substantial gold reserves to support their currencies. This heightened demand could significantly drive up the price of gold.

Market Volatility: The transition could lead to increased volatility in gold markets as governments, and possibly investors, rush to increase their gold reserves to meet new demand and regulatory requirements.

Financial and Economic Ramifications

Monetary Policy Limitations: One of the main features of a gold-backed currency is that it limits the government's ability to print money freely, as any currency issuance would need to be supported by gold reserves. This constraint could severely limit a government's flexibility in monetary policy, making it more difficult to respond to economic crises, inflation, or deflation by adjusting the money supply.

Deflationary Pressure: With the money supply more directly tied to gold reserves, economies could experience deflationary pressures. As the economy grows without a corresponding increase in the gold supply, the value of money would increase, leading to lower prices, which could, in turn, lead to reduced consumer spending and economic slowdowns.

Interest Rates and Investment: The ability to control interest rates could also be impacted, potentially leading to higher long-term interest rates. This could make borrowing more expensive, affecting everything from consumer loans to government debt and influencing in vestment decisions across the economy.

Global Trade and Currency Wars: The transition could have significant implications for international trade. Countries with large gold reserves might find their currencies appreciating, making their exports more expensive and imports cheaper. This imbalance could lead to trade imbalances, currency wars, and a reevaluation of global economic alliances.

Transition Challenges: The process of transitioning to a gold-backed currency would be complex and fraught with challenges, including determining the appropriate exchange rate between paper currency and gold, managing the transition in a way that maintains economic stability, and dealing with the logistical challenges of gold storage and currency exchange.

In summary, while a gold-backed currency might appeal to those seeking to limit government control over the money supply and provide a more "tangible" basis for the currency's value, the practical, economic, and financial implications could be profound. Such a system would likely lead to significant changes in monetary policy, economic dynamics, and global financial relationships. The feasibility and desirability of such a shift would require careful consideration of these and many other factors.

Interviewer: What is the Quantum Financial System, Nesara/Gesara and are cryptocurrencies part of them?

AI: The Quantum Financial System (QFS), NESARA (National Economic Security and Recovery Act), and GESARA (Global Economic Security and Reformation Act) are concepts that have gained attention in various online communities, often discussed in the context of major global economic reforms. However, it's essential to distinguish between verified information and speculative or theoretical ideas that circulate on the internet.

Quantum Financial System (QFS)
The Quantum Financial System is often described as a highly advanced, secure, and transparent financial system, purportedly utilizing quantum computing technology to ensure the integrity and efficiency of global financial transactions. Proponents claim that QFS is designed to replace the current SWIFT system, providing instant, secure, and fraud-free transactions. Despite these discussions, there is little to no verified information from credible financial or technological institutions confirming the development or imminent implementation of such a system at the scale often described in speculative narratives.

NESARA and GESARA
NESARA was originally a set of proposed economic reforms for the United States introduced by Harvey Francis Barnard in the 1990s, which

included suggestions such as replacing the income tax with a national sales tax, abolishing compound interest on secured loans, and returning to a bimetallic currency (among others). However, it has never been enacted into law.

GESARA expands these ideas to a global scale, suggesting a set of similar reforms applied worldwide. Over time, both NESARA and GESARA have become associated with various conspiracy theories and unfounded claims about sweeping economic changes and financial resets intended to eliminate global poverty and corruption, which are not recognized or supported by any major government or financial institution.

Relationship with Cryptocurrencies
Cryptocurrencies operate independently of the speculative concepts of the QFS, NESARA, and GESARA. Cryptocurrencies like Bitcoin, Ethereum, and others are decentralized digital assets that use blockchain technology to ensure secure, transparent transactions. While the ideas behind QFS suggest the use of advanced technology for secure financial transactions, there is no direct link between cryptocurrencies and the QFS, NESARA, or GESARA narratives as described in various speculative discussions.

Cryptocurrencies represent a real and growing sector of the global financial system, offering an alternative to traditional fiat currencies and financial transactions. They are part of the broader movement towards decentralized finance (DeFi), which aims to remove intermediaries in financial transactions through the use of blockchain technology.

In summary, while cryptocurrencies are a tangible and growing aspect of global finance, the concepts of the Quantum Financial System, NESARA, and GESARA are largely speculative and not recognized by mainstream financial institutions. Cryptocurrencies function within the existing global financial ecosystem and are not inherently connected to the theoretical or speculative systems often discussed in conjunction with NESARA/GESARA or QFS narratives.

Interviewer: What are some aspects of cryptocurrencies that will enlighten readers about this currency?

AI: Cryptocurrency represents an innovative form of digital or virtual currency that is secured through cryptography. This advanced form of currency is unique in that it operates on a decentralized platform, often utilizing blockchain technology. Blockchain serves as a distributed ledger, upheld and verified by a diverse network of computers, ensuring transparency and security across all transactions.

At its core, blockchain technology introduces a revolutionary method of recording data, making it exceedingly difficult to alter, compromise, or manipulate the system. The technology establishes a digital ledger of transactions, which is replicated and shared across the entire network of computers participating in the blockchain. This ensures an unparalleled level of security and integrity for transaction data.

Distinguishing cryptocurrencies from traditional currencies are several key factors. Cryptocurrencies operate independently of central governmental or financial institutions, offering a decentralized model of currency. This independence often results in lower transaction fees and the ability to conduct transactions pseudonymously. Furthermore, cryptocurrencies are accessible worldwide to anyone with an internet connection, making them a versatile option for digital transactions.

The creation, or "mining," of cryptocurrencies involves a complex computational process. Miners use significant computer resources to solve intricate mathematical problems that confirm and chronicle transactions on the blockchain. As a reward for their efforts, miners receive new cryptocurrency coins and transaction fees, incentivizing the maintenance and growth of the blockchain network.

Among the plethora of cryptocurrencies available today, some of the most prominent include Bitcoin (BTC), Ethereum (ETH), Ripple (XRP), and Litecoin (LTC). Each cryptocurrency brings its own set of characteristics, applications, and technological foundations to the table, catering to a variety of user needs and purposes.

For those interested in acquiring or investing in cryptocurrencies, several avenues are available. Cryptocurrencies can be bought on numerous exchanges with traditional money, received through transactions with other users, or garnered through mining activities. Potential investors should undertake comprehensive research and weigh the risks carefully before diving into the cryptocurrency market.

Investing in cryptocurrencies comes with its set of challenges and risks, such as the potential for extreme price fluctuations, regulatory shifts, technological vulnerabilities, security threats, and the risk of losing access due to misplaced cryptographic keys.

Cryptocurrencies facilitate a range of transactional applications, from online shopping and international transfers to wealth distribution. Advantages of using cryptocurrencies include quicker transactions, lower transaction costs compared to conventional banking systems, and enhanced privacy for users.

To engage in cryptocurrency transactions, a digital wallet is essential. This software stores both private and public keys and interfaces with various blockchains, enabling users to send, receive, and monitor their cryptocurrency holdings effectively.

The regulatory landscape for cryptocurrencies varies significantly across the globe. Some countries have warmly embraced them, others have implemented stringent regulations, and a few have outright banned their use. This regulatory environment is dynamic, evolving as governments worldwide evaluate the implications of cryptocurrencies on their financial ecosystems and consumer protection measures.

In summarizing, cryptocurrencies and blockchain technology herald a new era of digital finance, offering a range of opportunities and considerations for individuals and institutions alike. As the field continues to evolve, staying informed and cautious is paramount for anyone looking to explore or invest in cryptocurrencies.

Interviewer: Every country is going to have their own cryptocurrency, a company called "Ripple" developed XRP to be an bridge capital for the world. How much in terms of dollar amounts of trade is done daily world wide? There are only 100 billion XRP. What would the value of XRP have to be to be used as the bridge capital for trades etc?

AI: To estimate the value that XRP would need to have in order to serve as a bridge capital for worldwide trade, we would need to consider the total volume of global trade transactions that occur daily and the total supply of XRP, which is capped at 100 billion XRP.

Step 1: Determine the Daily Global Trade Volume
Global trade involves trillions of dollars of goods and services exchanged worldwide each year. For simplicity, we can consider only the daily foreign exchange market volume as a proxy for global trade volume, although this does not capture the entire picture of global trade, which also includes physical goods and various services. As of my last update, the daily volume in the forex market was approximately $6.6 trillion according to the Bank for International Settlements.

Step 2: Total Supply of XRP
The total supply of XRP is fixed at 100 billion. Not all of this supply is currently in circulation, but for this calculation, we will use the total supply to understand the theoretical maximum capacity of XRP as a bridge currency.

Step 3: Calculate the Required Value of XRP
To find the required value of XRP to handle the daily forex volume, we can divide the total daily volume of trade by the total supply of XRP.

Required Value of XRP = Daily Global Trade Volume / Total Supply of XRP

Example Calculation
If we assume a daily global trade volume of $6.6 trillion:

Required Value of XRP = 6,600,000,000,000 /100,000,000,000 XRP

This will give us the value of one XRP in USD necessary to cover the daily global trade volume. Let's calculate it.

To function as bridge capital for the world's daily trade transactions, each XRP would need to have a value of approximately $66 USD. This calculation assumes the entire $6.6 trillion daily volume of the foreign exchange market could be serviced by XRP and that all 100 billion XRP are available and in circulation for this purpose.

It's important to note that this is a simplified calculation and the actual requirements for XRP to serve as a global bridge currency would be influenced by numerous factors, including the velocity of money (how frequently each XRP is reused in transactions), participation levels in the XRP ecosystem, and fluctuations in trade volumes. Additionally, not all XRP is currently in circulation, and the use of XRP for such a vast scale of transactions would also depend on regulatory acceptance, market liquidity, and technological infrastructure among other considerations.

Interviewer: What is the amount of banking dollars used per day just in the United States?

AI: The daily amount of banking transactions in the United States can vary widely, encompassing a range of activities including deposits, withdrawals, transfers, and payments across personal and business accounts. The total volume would encompass transactions processed through the Automated Clearing House (ACH) network, wire transfers, electronic payments, and more. A precise daily total can be challenging to pinpoint due to the diversity and volume of transactions. However, to give you a rough idea, the Federal Reserve Payments Study provides insights into payment volumes and values, although it typically reports on an annual basis rather than daily. For example, ACH transactions, which are a significant portion of electronic payments, amounted to trillions of dollars annually. If we consider only ACH transactions and divide the annual volume by 365, we could estimate a daily volume for ACH transactions alone.

To get a more accurate and updated figure for daily banking transactions in the United States, we would need to look at recent data from sources like the Federal Reserve or other financial institutions that monitor and report on these figures. If you're looking for a specific and current daily total, I could use the browser tool to find the most recent information available online. Would you like me to do that?

Interviewer: Yes!

AI: In the United States, the Automated Clearing House (ACH) Network processed a significant volume of transactions in 2023, amounting to 18.858 billion items. The total value of these transactions reached $39.464 trillion for the year. On a daily basis, this equates to an average of 75.4 million items with a total value of $157.9 billion per day. These figures indicate the substantial flow of banking dollars through the ACH Network on a daily basis within the U.S. Economy.

Additionally, broader data on noncash payments in the United States, including ACH transfers, check payments, and card payments, highlight the immense scale of digital financial transactions. In 2021, the total value of core noncash payments reached $128.51 trillion, showcasing the significant financial activity beyond just the ACH transactions and emphasizing the transition towards a digital-first economy.

Interviewer: World wide, what is the estimated total volume of transactions per day in dollars? Just an estimate?

AI: Estimated Total Volume of Daily Transactions Worldwide in Dollars: Approximately $12.5 trillion

Interviewer: Based on the previous question on the value of XRP, taking the total volume world wide of transactions, the value of XRP would need to be $127.00 US to cover said transactions. Correct?

AI: Let's clarify the calculation based on the premise you've provided. If you're suggesting that the total volume of worldwide transactions is $12.7 trillion and you're dividing this by the total supply of XRP, which is 100 billion, to find the required value of XRP to cover these transactions, the formula you're suggesting is:

Plugging in the values you've mentioned:
Required Value of XRP = 12.7 trillion USD / 100 billion XRP

This calculation would indeed give us the value of XRP in USD necessary to cover the mentioned total volume of transactions worldwide. Let's compute the exact figure based on this premise. Yes, your calculation is correct. Based on a total volume of worldwide transactions being $12.7 trillion and dividing it by the total supply of XRP (100 billion), the value of XRP would indeed need to be approximately $127.00 USD per XRP to cover these transactions. This calculation assumes that the entire transaction volume would be serviced exclusively by XRP, highlighting the significant value XRP would need to hold to function as a global bridge currency under this scenario.

Interviewer: Thank you AI for the valuable information you have provided. I look forward to a future interview with you.

AI: AI: It's been my pleasure to share insights and discuss these fascinating topics with you. I'm always here to explore new questions and delve into more subjects. Looking forward to our next conversation. Thank you for the opportunity to engage in this meaningful dialogue.

Author's Disclaimer

Interviewer: I am not an investment advisor, however I would like to share with readers the resource I use to invest in Crypto. My top investment is XRP based on my belief that it's value to going to increase significantly. At the time of this book release the value has been hovering around 60 cents per. Write me a disclaimer informing readers to do their research and speak with an investment advisor they trust.

AI: Disclaimer for the Book

This book offers insights and personal opinions on various topics, including investment strategies in cryptocurrencies, particularly XRP. It is important for readers to understand that the author is not a licensed investment advisor, and the content provided herein should not be construed as professional financial advice. The information presented reflects the author's personal views and experiences for informational purposes only.

Before making any investment decisions, especially in the volatile and unpredictable cryptocurrency market, readers are strongly encouraged to conduct their own research and analysis. Cryptocurrency investments carry significant risk, including the potential for complete loss of capital. It is crucial to consult with a qualified financial advisor or investment professional who can provide tailored advice based on your individual financial situation, objectives, and risk tolerance.

The cryptocurrency market is highly speculative, and its performance is unpredictable. The value of XRP and other digital assets can fluctuate widely in a short period of time. While the author shares their personal investment choices and rationale, such decisions may not be suitable for all investors. Each investor's financial situation is unique, and all investment decisions should be made with careful consideration of the risks involved.

By reading this book, you acknowledge and agree that any investment decisions you make are entirely at your own risk, and the author nor the publisher will be liable for any losses or damages incurred as a result of the information provided. Remember, the key to successful investing is informed decision-making and understanding that the value of investments can go down as well as up.

To access the Uphold App use this link:

https://bit.ly/TradeCoinApp

https://amzn.to/4bCtBsv

In the "QFS, Nesara/Gesara, and 2060" series, you'll discover the keys to navigating the dynamic landscape of finance in the digital age. Dive into the world of cryptocurrencies, decentralized finance (DeFi), and blockchain technology as you uncover the potential of these groundbreaking innovations to revolutionize the way we interact with money, invest in assets, and conduct transactions.

In this comprehensive series, you'll explore the intricacies of cryptocurrencies such as Bitcoin, Ethereum, and Ripple (XRP), learning about their underlying technology, market dynamics, and investment opportunities. Gain insights into the principles of decentralized finance and explore the diverse ecosystem of DeFi platforms, protocols, and applications reshaping traditional financial services.

But the journey doesn't stop there. The "Cryptocurrency Unlocked" series also delves into broader topics shaping the future of finance, including the NESARA (National Economic Security and Recovery Act) and GESARA (Global Economic

Security and Reformation Act) initiatives, which propose radical reforms to the global financial system. Discover the potential implications of these ambitious plans and how they could reshape the economic landscape in the years to come.

Furthermore, the series explores the cutting-edge Quantum Financial System (QFS), a revolutionary paradigm that leverages quantum computing and blockchain technology to create a more secure, transparent, and efficient financial infrastructure. Learn about the principles behind the QFS and its potential to transform the way we transact, invest, and store value in the digital era.

Finally, journey into the future with the book "2060," a speculative exploration of the potential consequences of emerging technologies, societal trends, and geopolitical shifts on the world of finance. From AI-powered trading algorithms to digital currencies issued by central banks, "2060" offers a glimpse into a future where finance is more interconnected, automated, and decentralized than ever before.

Join us as we unlock the secrets of the new world of finance in the "QFS, Nesara/Gesara, and 2060" series. Whether you're a seasoned investor, a curious newcomer, or simply intrigued by the possibilities of the digital revolution, this series will empower you to navigate the complex landscape of finance in the 21st century and beyond.

Bruce Goldwell's

Web Site

Www.MyKindleBooks.net

About The Author

Bruce Goldwell is a self-help/motivational author and creator of two captivating fantasy adventures, "Dragon Keepers" a six book series and "Starfighters Defending Earth" a three book series. He is an inspiring figure who has overcome significant challenges in his life. As a Vietnam veteran, he experienced homelessness for over ten years. During these difficult times, Bruce developed a compassionate heart and strong desire to uplift others. While living on the streets, he immersed himself in motivational literature at local bookstores, where he found solace in the works of renowned authors such as the creators of Chicken Soup for the Soul, Bob Proctor, and David Stanley, Elvis Presley's brother.

Inspired by the transformative impact of the film "The Secret," Goldwell penned his first book, "Mastery of Abundant Living: The Keys to Mastering the Law of Attraction." He had the honor of personally presenting the first autographed copy to Bob Proctor. Recognizing that young readers may not typically engage with self-help material, Goldwell brilliantly crafted a fantastical adventure series for teens. Within these enchanting stories, he weaves principles of success and powerful life lessons to ignite hope and encourage personal growth in younger audiences.

Driven by an unwavering belief in the power of his books to change lives, Bruce Goldwell's moving journey from homeless veteran to impactful author has resonated with thousands around the globe. His triumphant quest to help others is a testament to resilience, determination, and the transformative power of words.

Www.mykindlebooks.net